Portugal

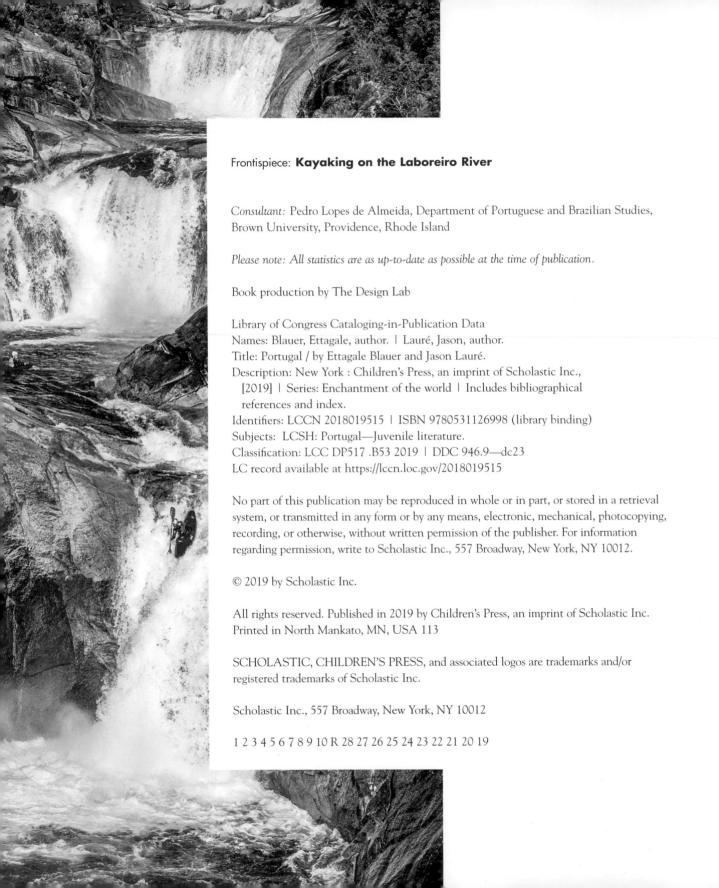

Frontispiece: **Kayaking on the Laboreiro River**

Consultant: Pedro Lopes de Almeida, Department of Portuguese and Brazilian Studies, Brown University, Providence, Rhode Island

Please note: All statistics are as up-to-date as possible at the time of publication.

Book production by The Design Lab

Library of Congress Cataloging-in-Publication Data
Names: Blauer, Ettagale, author. | Lauré, Jason, author.
Title: Portugal / by Ettagale Blauer and Jason Lauré.
Description: New York : Children's Press, an imprint of Scholastic Inc.,
  [2019] | Series: Enchantment of the world | Includes bibliographical
  references and index.
Identifiers: LCCN 2018019515 | ISBN 9780531126998 (library binding)
Subjects: LCSH: Portugal—Juvenile literature.
Classification: LCC DP517 .B53 2019 | DDC 946.9—dc23
LC record available at https://lccn.loc.gov/2018019515

Scholastic Inc., 557 Broadway, New York, NY 10012

1 2 3 4 5 6 7 8 9 10 R 28 27 26 25 24 23 22 21 20 19

Portugal

BY ETTAGALE BLAUER & JASON LAURÉ

Enchantment of the World™
Second Series

CHILDREN'S PRESS®

An Imprint of Scholastic Inc.

Contents

Left to right: **Porto, rock formations, spoonbill, Belém Tower, traditional jewelry**

CHAPTER I

Across the Seas

THERE IS A SAYING THAT GEOGRAPHY IS DESTINY. It means that a country's location, its neighbors, and the natural resources it enjoys shape the lives of the people who live there. That is certainly true of the nation of Portugal and the Portuguese people.

Portugal's physical position in the world set the stage for its history. The nation is located in western Europe. It is, in some ways, isolated. It sits on the southwestern corner of a promontory, a piece of land jutting out from the mainland. The mighty Atlantic Ocean stretches out to the west. Fierce winds from the Atlantic pummel the shoreline. Inland, mountain ranges separate different regions of the country, shaping the land and the lives of the people who live there.

Portugal's position on the edge of Europe encouraged the Portuguese people to look outside their own territory. Instead

Opposite: **Many towns and cities in Portugal hug the coastline.**

of closing itself off, explorers set out into the unknown, to seek out different lands around the world and encounter ideas new to them.

For some people, the vast ocean could seem like an obstacle that could not be overcome. But the Portuguese saw it as a challenge. The Portuguese first traveled out to the sea to fish to feed their families. Later, people began exploring farther down the coast. Over time, the mighty ocean encouraged the Portuguese to develop brilliant and brave sailors and explorers, mathematicians and mapmakers, and an adventurous spirit. Eventually, people from this tiny nation made their way around the world.

For people in the 1400s, crossing the ocean to find out what other lands existed was a dangerous endeavor. The world was largely unmapped and uncharted. The distant world was full of unknown weather, unknown mountains, unknown dangers. No one knew where the ocean ended and what they might find there. There was always the chance that the explorers would never make it back home. Yet something drove the Portuguese to take chances, to make the journey

Portuguese explorer Vasco da Gama led four ships around the Cape of Good Hope at the southern tip of Africa in 1497. Da Gama and his crew continued east to India, becoming the first Europeans to sail there.

Belém Tower was built as a fortress, guarding the entrance to the Tagus River.

Belém Tower

The Belém district of Lisbon is the site where Portuguese explorers set sail on their voyages. There, at the mouth of the Tagus River, King Manuel I built a series of grand monuments and a church to celebrate those successful sailors. Belém Tower and the Jerónimos Monastery were built under his guidance in what is now called the Manueline style of architecture.

The tower is elaborately decorated with stone carvings and balconies. Watchtowers peer out from the top corners of it. A large statue of the Virgin Mary and the baby Jesus on the tower offered protection for the sailors as they set out across the great ocean. Built between 1514 and 1520, it is one of the best-known monuments of the age of exploration.

into new places. They put tremendous faith in the scientists and mathematicians who gave them the tools to sail away from the coast of Portugal and seek new worlds.

These explorations changed the lives of millions of people around the world. The Portuguese traveled to Africa, South America, and Asia. They left a legacy of their language, their culture and their scientific achievements wherever they went.

Yet a large part of this legacy was destructive. As the Portuguese explored the world, they also colonized distant lands. They began trading enslaved people to work these lands. Millions of people were kidnapped along the coast of Africa. They were shipped across the ocean, never to be seen again by their families. Those Africans were taken thousands of miles away, mainly to Brazil in South America as well as to

Many Portuguese people trace their ancestry to the parts of Africa that Portugal once colonized.

Lisbon is a thriving city with a long history.

the Caribbean, North America, and Europe. The Portuguese believed that as white people they were superior to those they encountered around the world and that they had the right to claim distant lands as possessions. They also believed they had the right to use the labor of other people for their own country's profit.

This disruption of the lives of Africans, the forced movement of roughly ten million people into forced labor in other parts of the world, set the stage for many problems that remain today. Six centuries after the Portuguese started their maritime explorations in the 1400s, the consequences of their travels are with us every day.

Over time, all of the regions Portugal had claimed as colonies regained their freedom. Across the centuries, Portugal also remade itself. It has transformed from a monarchy into a republic. It joined the European Economic Community, now called the European Union, and met new obligations. It has absorbed immigrants from its former colonies and other parts of the world.

Recent decades have seen a huge shift in Portugal as it has accommodated these changes. Portugal has sometimes struggled economically and politically, but it has become a modern European country. This is the nation that we study today.

Portuguese boys enjoy a beautiful day at a beach near Lisbon.

CHAPTER 2

A Pleasant Land

PORTUGAL IS SITUATED IN THE SOUTHWESTERN COR-
ner of Europe. It occupies one-sixth of a large,
square-shaped piece of land called the Iberian Peninsula.
Spain makes up the remaining five-sixths of the peninsula.
Portugal's only land border is with Spain, which wraps around
Portugal on the north and east. Portugal's western and southern borders lie on the Atlantic Ocean. Because Portugal hugs
the ocean, being there sometimes gives a person the sense of
being at the end of the earth. This strong connection with the
ocean encouraged Portugal's prominence as a seagoing nation.
Fishing and sailing are important elements in the life and history of its people.

Portugal is a small nation. It measures just 350 miles (560
kilometers) from north to south and 140 miles (200 km) from
east to west. Its land area is 35,603 square miles (92,212 sq km),

Opposite: **Boats travel among the rock formations at Ponta da Piedade, in southern Portugal.**

Portugal's Geographic Features

Area: 35,603 square miles (92,212 sq km)

Highest Elevation: Mount Pico in the Azores, 7,713 feet (2,351 m)

Highest Elevation on the Mainland: Mount Torre, 6,539 feet (1,993 m)

Lowest Elevation: Sea level along the coast

Longest River Entirely within Portugal: Mondego, 137 miles (220 km)

Longest River: Tagus, 171 miles (275 km)

Average High Temperature: In Lisbon, 59°F (15°C) in January, 82°F (28°C) in July

Average Low Temperature: In Lisbon, 47°F (8°C) in January, 65°F (18°C) in July

Average Annual Precipitation: 20 to 80 inches (50 to 200 cm)

about the same size as the U.S. state of Indiana. This area includes two mountainous island groups in the Atlantic Ocean.

Houses sit among boulders atop the Estrela Mountains, the highest mountains on the Portuguese mainland.

The Lay of the Land

Although Portugal is small, its geographic regions are extremely varied. The landscape of the different regions has shaped the culture, farming, work, and foods of the people who live there.

In the north, the land is mountainous. The Larouco Mountains lie in the northwest. Rivers have rushed down these mountains over the millennia, leaving behind deep gorges. Farming is difficult in this area because the hillsides are strewn with large rocks. Farther inland in the north are high, rolling plateaus.

The nation's highest mountains on the mainland rise in the central part of the country. The highest peak, Mount Torre, in the Estrela Mountains, reaches 6,539 feet (1,993 meters) above sea level. Other mountain chains in central Portugal include the Montemuro and the Gardunha. In east-central Portugal, there are many small farms.

Portugal's largest rivers flow through the country's central region. The Douro marks central Portugal's northern boundary and the Tagus its southern boundary. Both the Douro and the Tagus begin in the mountains of Spain and flow west across

A kayaker braves the falls on the Laboreiro River, which tumbles down the mountains in northern Portugal.

Cabo da Roca is the most westerly spot in mainland Europe. The cliffs there rise about 460 feet (140 m) above the ocean.

The Place at the End of the World

A small mountain chain called the Sintra Mountains reaches the Atlantic coast not far from Lisbon. It ends at Cabo da Roca (Cape Roca), the westernmost point on the European continent. At Cabo da Roca, a dramatic cliff measuring 459 feet (140 m) rises nearly straight up from the waters below. A lighthouse stands on top of the cliff, shining a beacon through the fog that often blankets the area, to warn ships of the rocky coast. The cliff at Cabo da Roca is known as *fim do mundo*, "the place at the end of the world," because standing on that cliff, there is nothing to see but the vast, cold ocean.

Portugal. Farmers in the Douro Valley have carved small, flat terraces into the hillsides, where they plant grapes to make wine. The city of Porto is located where the Douro River flows into the ocean. Port wine is named after this city. Lisbon, the capital of Portugal and its largest city, lies near the mouth of the Tagus, which has an excellent natural harbor. Most of the nation's industry is near Lisbon. The Mondego, another river in the central part of the country, is the longest river entirely within Portugal.

The land father south in Portugal is called the Alentejo. It is a region covered by low hills and plains. The Alentejo is one of the driest areas in the nation. Farmers there raise crops that are suitable to the low rainfall, such as olives and cork. Some farmers also raise cattle in this region.

At the southern end of the nation, beyond a mountain range called the Caldeirão, is a region called the Algarve. This region escapes much of the harsher weather of other parts of Portugal and attracts many tourists to its sandy beaches.

In some parts of Algarve, in southern Portugal, wind and rain have eroded the dry land into magnificent shapes.

The Alqueva Dam blocks the flow of the Guadiana River, forming the largest lake in Portugal.

The Alqueva Dam

The availability of water is a key environmental issue for countries around the world. This has become even more of a concern as global climate change has upset usual weather patterns. In Portugal, the natural scarcity of water is a fact of life in the Algarve and Alentejo. As far back as the 1950s, the government of Portugal began to consider plans for a dam on the Guadiana River, in southern Portugal. Political upheavals kept the plans on hold. In the 1990s, the plan went ahead, and the nation embarked on this enormous building project. It was considered controversial because the dam would flood a village, an area with ancient artifacts and important wildlife habitat. The Alqueva Dam was completed in 2002. By damming the water from the river, a large reservoir was created. This was designed to help the region through years of drought. A power station, using the energy of the water flowing over the dam, was also built. This stores energy when demand is low and then releases it when demand is high.

In the southeast of Portugal is the Guadiana River, which marks part of the border between Portugal and Spain. It flows south, eventually entering the Gulf of Cádiz, an arm of the Atlantic Ocean.

Islands

Two archipelagos, or chains of islands, are part of the Portuguese nation: the Azores and Madeira.

The Azores, which lie about 800 miles (1,300 km) west of the coast of Portugal, are the remnants of ancient volcanoes. They are located at the junction of three tectonic plates, giant pieces of earth's outer layer that fit together like puzzle pieces. At the edges of the tectonic plates, molten rock from deep underground has more places it can escape to the surface, so volcanic activity is more common. The active underground

Men on the island of São Miguel in the Azores pull a pot filled with stew from a hole in the ground where it has cooked from the natural heat beneath the earth. This area, known as the Furnace, is peppered with hot springs, boiling mud, and places where steam escapes the ground.

The earthquake produced a tsunami with waves 20 feet (6 m) high in Lisbon and three times that height in Spain.

The Great Lisbon Earthquake

The most devastating earthquake in the history of Portugal leveled Lisbon in 1755. A series of violent quakes on the morning of November 1 destroyed many buildings, but that was only the beginning of the disaster. The quakes produced a tsunami, a massive ocean wave, that flooded parts of the city. The shaking and the floods produced fires that engulfed what remained of the city. By the time it was all over, almost every building in the city had been destroyed. Tens of thousands of people had been killed, making it one of the deadliest quakes in history. Lisbon has not suffered another major earthquake since 1755, but small quakes shake the city regularly.

world beneath the Azores is apparent in the many hot springs on the islands. The heat underground warms water that bubbles up through cracks. Some people in the Azores also cook with the underground heat. They put meat and vegetables in a pot and then bury it. Several hours later, they retrieve the pot and enjoy a perfectly cooked stew.

In the Azores, many crater lakes have formed on the top of extinct volcanoes.

Steep, rugged mountains dominate the Azores. The highest point in all of Portugal is Mount Pico, located on Pico Island. It rises to 7,713 feet (2,351 m). Many of the peaks in the Azores are topped by calderas, the craters left behind after volcanic explosions. Over thousands of years, these craters filled with water to form lakes.

The Azores were uninhabited until Portuguese sailors discovered them in 1427. About a quarter-million people live in the Azores today, and it is possible to fly directly to the Azores from major cities around the world.

The Madeira archipelago lies about 650 miles (1,000 km) southwest of Portugal. Like the Azores, it is volcanic in origin. The islands are rugged, with cliffs rising from the coasts. About 290,000 people live in the archipelago, the vast majority on Madeira Island.

Climate

Weather varies greatly along the length of Portugal with the north generally being colder than the south. In general, the interior parts of the country experience the highest temperatures, while the coastal areas are most pleasant. It never gets extremely cold. Even in the northern region, where snow sometimes falls on the highest mountain peaks, temperatures rarely drop below freezing. The farther south you go, the warmer it gets until you reach the sun-drenched Algarve.

The hottest area is the Alentejo, where summer

Much of the land on Madeira is covered with ancient rain forests.

A shepherd leads his flock to grazing land on a snowy day in the mountains of northern Portugal.

temperatures can top 110 degrees Fahrenheit (43 degrees Celsius). The pleasant Algarve receives cooling breezes from the ocean, and although it's sunny all day long, the temperature rarely exceeds 85°F (29°C).

Northern parts of the country receive the most rain. Some parts of the northwest receive 80 inches (200 centimeters) of rain per year. The Algarve, on the other hand, gets only about 20 inches (50 cm) of rain per year. This region receives almost no rain in the summer months.

Urban Landscapes

More than half of Portugal's people live in cities and the suburbs around them. Each city has a distinct personality that reflects its terrain and settlers. The nation's largest city is its capital, Lisbon. About 500,000 people live in Lisbon, but there are nearly 3 million people in the urban area that includes the city and the surrounding area.

The nation's second-largest city is Porto, home to about 250,000 people. Porto, located where the Douro River meets the ocean, has played a major role in Portugal's history. The Romans used it as a trading post some two thousand years ago. It was a center of trade for each wave of migrants who passed through. It is known for its beautiful cathedral and the São Bento Railway Station, which features incredible murals of the history of Portugal made from traditional blue-and-white tiles called azulejos. Today, manufacturing, fishing, and tourism are all important to the city's economy.

The stairway leading up to Bom Jesus do Monte in Braga has 577 steps.

With a population of about 120,000, Braga is the nation's fourth-largest city. Braga lies in the north of the country. One of the nation's oldest cities, Braga was founded roughly 2,300 years ago. Its twelfth-century cathedral is the oldest in the country. Other important sites include the Braga Castle and a hilltop church called Bom Jesus do Monte. The city is a center for education and transportation.

The nation's third- and fifth-largest cities, Amadora and Setúbal, respectively, are both suburbs of Lisbon. Home to about 180,000 people, Amadora is mainly a residential city. It is Portugal's most densely populated city. Setúbal, south of the Tagus, is a major port city. It is home to about 117,000 people.

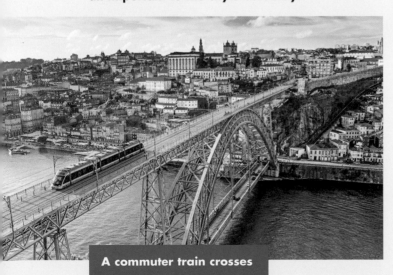

A commuter train crosses the Douro River in Porto.

CHAPTER 3

The Natural World

THE LAND AND CLIMATE OF PORTUGAL ARE VARIED, from the damp mountains of the north to the dry plains of the south to the lush remote islands. These regions include wildly diverse habitats where different kinds of plants and animals live.

Plant Life

Most of the land that is now Portugal was once covered in forest. But today, only about a quarter of the land is forested. Much of the land has been turned into vineyards, orchards, and farm fields. Common native trees include pines, oaks, and chestnuts. In the dryer areas, scrub juniper grows. The island of Madeira is famed for its laurel forests, which thrive in areas with mild, stable temperatures. Laurel forests are filled with evergreen plants with dark green, glossy leaves.

Opposite: **Wild Sorraia horses graze in the mountains of northwestern Portugal. Only a few hundred of these small, hardy horses remain.**

The Cork Oak

Portugal's national tree is the cork oak. This rugged evergreen tree is native to southwestern Europe and northwestern Africa. It has a thick, gray bark. For centuries, people have harvested the tree's bark and used the inner layer to make corks for wine bottles. This inner layer of cork is also used to make flooring and other goods. The bark can be stripped off roughly every ten years without harming the tree. Unlike many trees, the cork oak can regrow its bark.

Nearly a quarter of the forest that remains in Portugal consists of eucalyptus trees, which are native to Australia. These trees are planted because they grow quickly and can then be harvested to make paper. Some regions of Portugal have been planted with trees that produce olives, almonds, and citrus fruits.

In the spring, the land in Portugal comes alive with wildflowers. There are azaleas, daffodils, and irises, rockrose, orchids, and crocuses. Lavender, a purple flowering plant used in cooking and in scents, is Portugal's unofficial national flower.

Wildlife

More than a hundred different mammal species live in Portugal. The largest predators are the Iberian wolf and the Iberian lynx, which is a member of the cat family. Both are highly endangered because of habitat loss. About three hundred Iberian wolves live in Portugal, in the northern part of the country. Only a few hundred Iberian lynx remain in a few isolated places in Portugal and Spain. These elegant cats prey almost entirely on rabbits.

A more common predator is the red fox, which eats small mammals, birds, and insects. The fox is an omnivore, meaning

Lynx are easily identified by the tufts of black hair on the tops of their ears.

The Deadliest Fire

Wildfires are common in Portugal. In many years, more acres burned in tiny Portugal than in all the rest of Europe. But 2017 was a particularly bad year for fires. In June, fires roared through central Portugal. More than sixty people were killed, many trapped in their cars by the swift-moving fires. They were the deadliest forest fires in Portugal's history.

The blazes began when lightning struck land parched by summer heat. They spread quickly because the land was planted with eucalyptus trees, which are not native to the region. The sap in eucalyptus trees burns easily and shoots burning bark off the tree, which starts additional fires nearby. Trees native to Portugal, such as cork oak, are much more resistant to fire.

The Portuguese government has banned the planting of more eucalyptus trees. But the tree spreads easily, and in recent years Portugal has experienced increasingly hot and dry summers. Many people fear that ferocious fires will continue to be a problem.

Portuguese firefighters battle wildfires in June 2017. About 270 people were killed or injured in the fires.

it eats all kinds of food, so fruit such as berries, plums, and acorns are also a major part of its diet. The fox is highly adaptable and usually lives in forests and farmlands, but sometimes ventures into towns.

Other large animals found in Portugal include boars, deer, and wild goats. There are also many smaller creatures such as hedgehogs, shrews, and weasels.

Many mammals are found in the waters near Portugal. Whales and dolphins can be seen leaping above the water offshore, while seals sometimes pull themselves onto the rocks. The islands are particularly rich in marine mammals. The Azores are considered one of the world's great whale watching sites. Sperm whales, humpbacks, minkes, fins, and even blue whales, the largest creature on earth, are frequently spotted. Madeira is one of the few places where the endangered Mediterranean monk seal still lives.

A sperm whale dives near a tourist boat off the coast of the Azores. Sperm whales grow longer than a school bus.

Helpful Companions

Several dog breeds originated in Portugal. The Portuguese water dog is a close cousin of the poodle. Like the poodle, it is intelligent and hardworking. Portuguese water dogs are easy to train and eager to please. They were once common along the Portuguese coast, where they would plunge into the ocean to

A Portuguese water dog leaps into the sea.

Estrela mountain dogs were traditionally used by farmers to guard herds of sheep.

help retrieve fishing nets and carry messages between ships. Their waterproof coats and webbed feet are ideal for these tasks. The Portuguese water dog is a large creature, weighing up to 60 pounds (27 kilograms).

Even larger is the Estrela mountain dog, which sometimes reaches 130 pounds (60 kg). These dogs were bred to be herd dogs and guard dogs in the Estrela Mountains. Their thick coat keeps them warm in the cool mountain air. These majestic dogs are known for being alert, intelligent, and brave.

Crabs, clams, and oysters are common along the coast. A wide variety of fish live in the ocean waters, including sardines, tuna, and mackerel.

Portugal is rich in birdlife, in part because it is a convenient stopover for many birds migrating from northern Europe to Africa. Flamingos, spoonbills, ibises, egrets, and other long-legged birds feed in shallow waters, while eagles and kites soar overhead. Hoopoes search for insects along the dry ground, bluethroats linger in forests, and shearwaters fly low over the water before diving deep for fish.

Protected Lands

Since most of the people of Portugal live in the cities, there is an abundant amount of land that either is used for agriculture or has been set aside for nature parks. The Portuguese are

The spoonbill feeds by slightly opening its long bill and swinging it slowly through shallow water. When it comes across a fish or other creature, it snaps its bill shut.

Animals from Ancient Times

Long before there were any human beings on earth, there were dinosaurs. Just north of Lisbon, many dinosaur fossils have been discovered. The dinosaur fossils are on display at the Museum of Lourinhã, in the town of the same name. The region is now recognized as the most important dinosaur site in all of Europe. The specimens on display, thought to be 150 million years old, are helping scientists understand how the land of Europe developed.

A reconstructed skull of a Torvosaurus at the Museum of Lourinhã. The Torvosaurus was the largest predatory dinosaur known to roam Europe.

careful caretakers of the land. Over the centuries, they have learned to nurture the natural landscape and make good use of their fishing areas and farmland.

Although Portugal has many areas where natural landscapes are protected, it has only one national park. Peneda-Gerês National Park is located in the rugged northwest region of the country, next to the border with Spain. The park is known for its rocky landscape, refreshing waterfalls, soaring eagles, wild ponies, and the rare sighting of wolves. The park also protects the remains of buildings dating as far back as the Roman era. Villagers have traditionally spent part of the year living in stone houses in the park. This practice continues to this day.

The Tagus Estuary Natural Reserve was created to protect salt marshes and the waters of the Tagus River. It is a vital wintering area for waterbirds. Thousands of avocets, ducks, flamingos, and other birds can be seen there.

Portugal's highest peak on the mainland is found in Serra da Estrela Natural Park. Nature areas near the sea, including the Southwest Alentejo and Vicentine Coast Natural Park and São Jacinto Dunes Natural Reserve, offer a chance to experience pristine beaches, cliffs, and sand dunes.

Stone buildings for storing grain are among the historical treasures protected in Peneda-Gerês National Park. The buildings date to the eighteenth century.

CHAPTER 4

From Ancient to Modern

OVER THE COURSE OF THOUSANDS OF YEARS, WAVES of invaders and settlers washed over the land now called Portugal. Sitting on the edge of western Europe, not far from North Africa, it was a tempting target for people of other cultures. The Iberian Peninsula, now home to the nations of Spain and Portugal, was conquered by outsiders as far back as 1000 BCE.

Among the earliest to arrive were the Phoenicians, people based in the eastern Mediterranean. They were known for their sailing skills, which helped guide them to the southern coast of the Iberian Peninsula.

Other groups who arrived included the Celts, the Romans, the Vandals, the Visigoths, and the Moors. Each group brought its own culture and made its own contributions to what is now Portuguese culture.

Opposite: **The Moorish Castle sits high on a hilltop north of Lisbon. Moors, people from North Africa who had conquered the region, built it in the eighth and ninth centuries.**

Prehistoric people built thousands of stone structures in what is now Portugal. This dolmen, which marks the entryway to a tomb, is four to five thousand years old.

Celts and Romans

More than two thousand years ago, Celtic people migrated from central Europe to the Iberian Peninsula. In what is now Portugal, they merged with the local people, known as the Lusitani.

Roman armies first invaded the Iberian Peninsula in the third century BCE. The Romans took over the southern part of the peninsula. In the west, a Lusitani leader named Viriathus led the rebellion against the Romans. The Lusitani and other local groups succeeded in resisting the Romans until Viriathus was killed in 140 BCE. In 27 BCE, Lusitania, which encompasses much of today's Portugal and part of Spain, became a Roman province. Portugal's largest Roman settlement, Conímbriga, near today's Coimbra, was home to more than ten thousand people.

During their centuries in the Iberian Peninsula, the Romans built many grand structures, and some of their bridges and temples still stand. A more central influence was their language, Latin, which became the basis for the Portuguese language.

Roman rule in the Iberian Peninsula came to an end in the early 400s CE, when Germanic tribes invaded. Power changed hands several times, and by 700, a group known as the Visigoths ruled the entire peninsula. But soon, a new group would arrive that would have a much greater influence on the region.

Enter the Moors

In the year 711, Berber armies arrived on the Iberian Peninsula from North Africa. Berber people on the Iberian Peninsula are

The remains of a Roman temple constructed two thousand years ago still stand in Évora, in southern Portugal.

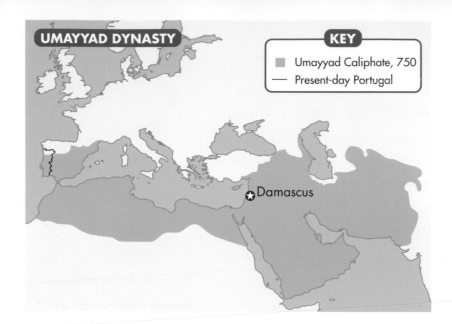

KEY
■ Umayyad Caliphate, 750
— Present-day Portugal

Damascus

known as Moors. Within a few months, they had defeated the Visigoths.

The Berbers were Muslim, followers of the religion Islam. They were part of the Umayyad dynasty, a great Muslim empire based in Damascus, Syria.

With the successful invasion, all of the Iberian Peninsula soon fell under the rule of the Umayyad dynasty. But in the decades that followed, the Umayyad leaders faced uprisings in North Africa and Asia. In 750, they were overthrown by the Abbasid dynasty. Many leaders of the Umayyad family were killed. But one, Abd al-Rahman, escaped to the Iberian Peninsula, where he established himself as the leader of the Umayyad dynasty there.

The Moors brought more than their religion. Because of centuries of Moorish rule, Islamic architecture and design can be seen in Portugal, especially in the southern part of the country. The Moors built schools and libraries. Their knowledge of science and engineering changed Portugal. Their music, philosophy, food, and language have had an enduring influence.

Religious fervor has been a driving force throughout history, and the Iberian Peninsula became a battleground for competing armies backing different religions. By the eleventh century, the Moors were being pushed out by people from Christian kingdoms to the north.

Centuries of Kings

The beginnings of modern Portugal took shape around this time when a small territory known by its Roman name, Portucale, was declared independent by its ruler, King Afonso Henriques, in 1143. For nearly eight hundred years, Portugal was ruled by a monarch. The Portuguese monarchs are called hereditary rulers because power passed from one generation to the next. They were not elected by anyone. They did, however, fight hard to keep control over the land they inherited.

Abd al-Rahman III ruled the Umayyad dynasty on the Iberian Peninsula for a half century. During his reign, its capital, Córdoba, in what is now Spain, became a great center of learning.

The Era of Exploration

When Portuguese kings began to feel secure in their own territory, they started to look beyond their own shores. The Portuguese were interested in exploring Europe to expand their scientific knowledge. They were also interested in the spice trade with Asia. Up to this point, all trade with people in the Far East involved long trips overland. Finally, the Portuguese wanted to spread the Christian faith.

Prince Henry the Navigator was a great supporter of Portugal's voyages of discovery. A son of King John I, who ruled

Henry the Navigator (center) studies a map. He sponsored explorations along the west coast of Africa.

The Portuguese developed the caravel in the 1400s.

The Perfect Ship

The best sailors in the world are only as good as their ships. The Portuguese had caravels, the very best ships of their day. The caravel is a small sailing ship that is easy to maneuver along the coastline and out into the ocean. Its sails are designed for speed and for sailing into the wind. The Portuguese shipbuilders based their design on Portuguese fishing boats and Islamic vessels used at that time.

These ships were small by modern standards, carrying no more than twenty sailors. The entire ship was about one-third the length of the wingspan of a modern 747 jet airplane, typically measuring just 75 feet (23 m) long. Different types of sails were used depending on the type of voyage. On the open sea, the sails were rigged fairly low to keep the ship from becoming hard to handle in rough weather. The design was so successful it allowed Portuguese explorers to cross the tremendous expanse of the Atlantic Ocean.

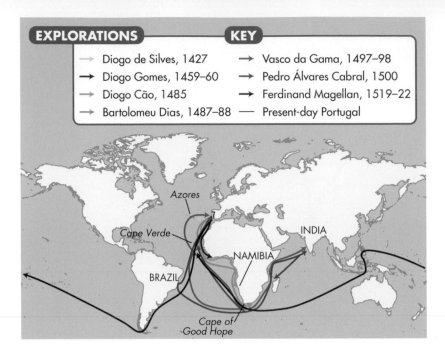

EXPLORATIONS | KEY

→ Diogo de Silves, 1427
→ Diogo Gomes, 1459–60
→ Diogo Cão, 1485
→ Bartolomeu Dias, 1487–88
→ Vasco da Gama, 1497–98
→ Pedro Álvares Cabral, 1500
→ Ferdinand Magellan, 1519–22
— Present-day Portugal

in the late 1300s and early 1400s, Henry had vast amounts of money to spend, and he used it to finance the expeditions. Prince Henry consulted with the best experts in geography, mapmaking, astronomy, and math. The results of all this work would soon be seen in the voyages of Portugal's best-known explorers.

In 1415, explorers ventured down the Portuguese coast

Portuguese Voyages in the Age of Discovery

1427 **Diogo de Silves reaches the Azores.**

1460 **Diogo Gomes discovers the Cape Verde archipelago.**

1485 **Diogo Cão reaches what is now Namibia, along the southwestern coast of Africa.**

1488 **Bartolomeu Dias sails around the Cape of Good Hope, the southern tip of Africa.**

1498 **Vasco da Gama reaches India.**

1500 **Pedro Álvares Cabral reaches what is now Brazil, in South America.**

1519–1522 **Ferdinand Magellan leads the first expedition around the globe. He dies in 1521, but one ship completes the voyage.**

and then to North Africa, where they captured the town of Ceuta in the region that would become Morocco. This gave Portugal a foothold in the middle of the Islamic world. Soon, Portuguese sailors were traveling far from their shores, first along the west African coast and then farther and farther away from Europe. They were aided by brilliant navigation tools such as the astrolabe. This small device gave the sailors a way to figure out where they were in relation to the constellations in the sky.

Among the many Portuguese explorers, Bartolomeu Dias stands out for his willingness to lead sailors to where no expedition had gone before. His travels along Africa's west and east coasts included navigating the wicked winds and surging seas

A portrait of Bartolomeu Dias holding an astrolabe

The Monument to the Discoveries features sculptures of thirty-three people who were central in Portugal's history of exploration.

Monument to the Discoveries

The Monument to the Discoveries commemorates key figures of Portugal's age of discovery. The monument is set on the Tagus River waterfront in the Belém neighborhood of Lisbon, and offers a dramatic history lesson for all to see. The sculpture stands 170 feet (52 m) high. It is shaped like a caravel, the sailing ship that made it possible for Portuguese sailors to travel around the world. Prince Henry the Navigator stands prominently at the very front of the ship.

Important explorers stand behind him, including Vasco da Gama, Pedro Álvares Cabral, Ferdinand Magellan, and Diogo Cão. All played roles in shaping the world. In addition to the explorers, the monument includes the figures of Luís de Camões, one of Portugal's most famous poets, as well as mapmakers and Portuguese kings. The monument was built in 1960, the five-hundredth anniversary of the death of Henry the Navigator.

at the very southern tip of Africa, then known as the Cape of Storms. Now it is called the Cape of Good Hope.

After Dias came Vasco da Gama who sailed all the way to India, and Ferdinand Magellan, who led an expedition around the globe. These voyages would change the cultural and political structure of the world.

Claiming Colonies

As Portuguese sailors reached distant lands, they claimed them for their country. In this way, Portugal amassed a global empire. Portuguese explorations and colonization

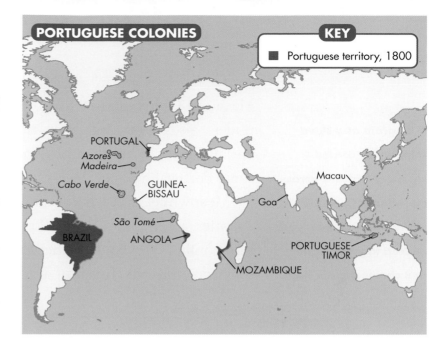

of distant lands spread the Portuguese language around the world. It also marked a period in which the Portuguese captured and enslaved others. The enslaved people enabled Portugal to benefit from the riches of these distant lands.

Most of Portugal's claims began as trading posts giving Portugal economic control. Portugal claimed Madeira in 1419 and the Azores Islands in 1427. Until the Portuguese arrived, these islands were uninhabited. Sailing along the African coast in the late 1400s sailors encountered Angola and Guinea-Bissau. Sailing around the Cape of Good Hope on the southern tip of Africa, they claimed Mozambique on Africa's east coast. The Portuguese continued into the Indian Ocean, searching for one of the most precious cargoes of the day: spices.

The Colonial Era

As Portugal expanded its influence in the world, it established profitable colonies in Brazil, in the Goa region of India, in

A diagram of a slave ship, which carried enslaved Africans across the Atlantic Ocean. On many ships, people were packed together tightly and chained to the floor.

Macau in China, and in parts of Southeast Asia. Portuguese traders also began supplying many of their colonies with enslaved people captured in Africa. Within a short period of time, Portugal became the biggest slave trader in the world.

Meanwhile, other European nations were also acquiring colonies around the world. Portugal and Spain soon came into conflict over lands in the Western Hemisphere. In 1494, they agreed to the Treaty of Tordesillas, which in effect gave

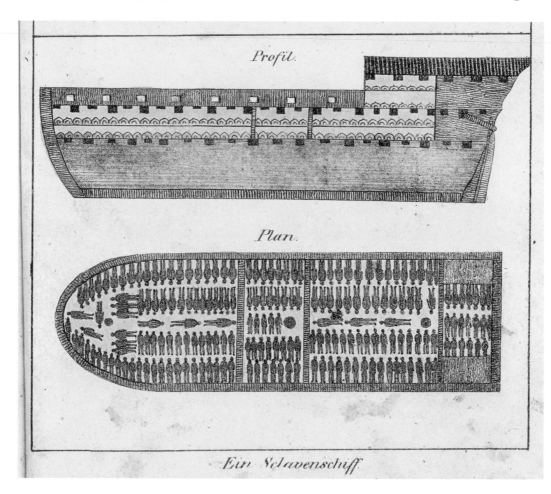

Profil.

Plan.

Ein Sclavenschiff.

Portugal claim to the western part of South America, and Spain claim to the rest of it.

The people who already lived in the areas that Portuguese explorers were encountering were not happy about being colonized by a foreign power. The first of Portugal's colonies to break away was the largest—Brazil. It declared independence in 1822.

In other parts of the world, however, European empires continued to grow. In 1884–1885, the European powers held a conference to settle their disputes over claims in Africa. Although Portugal tried to claim an enormous part of the African continent, stretching from the Atlantic Ocean to the Indian Ocean, the other European nations recognized Portugal's control over only the African territories of Angola,

Brazil declared its independence from Portugal in 1822 in what is known as the Cry of Ipiranga. Its war for independence would last two more years.

Portuguese colonists in Lourenço Marques in the early 1900s. The city is now called Maputo and is the capital of Mozambique.

Mozambique, Guinea, Cabo Verde, and São Tomé and Príncipe.

Portugal's struggle to keep the colonies continued into the twentieth century. In spite of its vast colonial possessions, Portugal was a poor country. It was ruled by hereditary kings, with power passed along from father to son. Some of the kings ruled well, but others squandered their power and wealth.

The First Republic

The Portuguese monarchy was weak. The kings' weakness gave birth to a group known as the Republicans, who were afraid that Portugal was going to be taken over by another European power. The kings had to give up the idea of Portugal remaining a monarchy. In 1908, King Charles I was murdered in Lisbon. Although the Portuguese were uncertain who had carried out the assassination, many Republicans supported it. King Charles's son, Manuel II, was just a teenager when he took the throne, and opposition to the monarchy grew stronger. In 1910, the Republicans forced elections to create a new form of government. It was called the First Republic.

The new leadership, however, was unstable. Between 1910 and 1926 Portugal had forty-five governments. One group would take over the parliament and then fail, over and over again. Even with the best of intentions, the governments had no money to make good on their promises to the people.

Portuguese cheer after the monarchy was overthrown in the revolution of 1910.

The Salazar Regime

After years of chaos, in 1926 the military seized power in a coup. In 1928, the military leaders appointed António de Oliveira Salazar minister of finance. A professor of economics, he worked to improve the nation's financial conditions. His power quickly grew, as conservatives, monarchists, business leaders, and others lined up behind him. In 1932, he was appointed prime minister.

Under a new constitution in 1933, Salazar became the dictator of what was called the Estado Novo, or the New State. He is often said to have ruled with an iron fist because he kept such firm control over people's lives.

Not all members of the Portuguese military supported the coup of 1926. Here, blindfolded officers who led a failed effort to oust the military government are brought to the army headquarters in Porto.

António de Oliveira Salazar ruled Portugal for thirty-six years.

Although the cost of the Portuguese colonies was one of the main reasons Portugal fell into debt, Salazar insisted on keeping a firm hold on the colonies because he considered them important to the growth of the Portuguese economy. While other European nations were letting go of their colonies, Salazar insisted the colonies were good for Portugal.

Political parties were banned in Portugal, and censorship was rampant. The people were unable to express their complaints. Living in Portugal and its colonies was like living in jail.

Portugal was one of the few nations in Europe that remained officially neutral in World War II, when the Allies,

World War II Hero

Aristides de Sousa Mendes was a Portuguese officer based in the consulate in Bordeaux, France, when Germany invaded France in 1940. Portugal was neutral in the war, siding neither with the Germans nor with the Americans and their allies.

As the German invasion advanced, thousands of people fled. Many were Jews who were likely to be murdered by the Nazi regime. The consulate headed by de Sousa Mendes was besieged by thousands of people seeking visas giving them permission to leave France. A visa from Portugal, with its neutral status, would allow them to travel to Lisbon and from there to safer parts of the world.

Portugal's prime minister, the dictator António de Oliveira Salazar, ordered Portuguese diplomats not to protect the refugees, especially Jewish people, and not to issue visas for their safe passage.

Aristides de Sousa Mendes (right) and Rabbi Chaim Kruger. Sousa Mendes carried out one of the largest rescue efforts of Jews by an individual during World War II.

Sousa Mendes had become friends with Chaim Kruger, a rabbi originally from Poland who was fleeing the Germans. He offered Kruger and his family visas. Kruger, however, refused to accept the visas unless all the other refugees in Bordeaux were also given visas. Sousa Mendes agreed. He immediately began issuing visas, thought to number around thirty thousand, within a few days. About ten thousand of the visas were issued to Jewish people.

Salazar was infuriated by this act of defiance. He stripped Sousa Mendes of everything he owned, leaving him and his family in complete poverty. Sousa Mendes was not honored for his heroism until after his death. Today, a street in Lisbon is named in his honor, as are other sites around the world.

including Great Britain and the United States, fought the Axis powers, led by Nazi Germany and Japan. Salazar played a key role in keeping Portugal out of World War II. He managed to help both the Allies and the Axis powers, giving aid to both sides, and in the process allowing Portugal to remain neutral. One of his most important deals was to trade a rare mineral called tungsten to the Germans for use in their weaponry. Tungsten hardens steel and allowed the Germans to make the best weapons. In exchange, they paid Portugal in millions of dollars that was worth tons of gold. During this same era,

A British armored car drives alongside an oxcart in the Azores in 1944. Both the United States and the United Kingdom used military bases on the Azores during World War II.

Remembering the Past

During the years of the Salazar dictatorship, many opponents of the regime were held in an old prison in the Alfama neighborhood of Lisbon. Today, that building is the Aljube Museum: Resistance and Freedom. (Aljube comes from the Arabic word for "prison.") One of Lisbon's newest museums, it opened in 2015.

The museum is meant to remind everyone of the Portuguese struggle for freedom. Three floors of exhibits tell the story of the New State's torture, oppression, and censorship. The museum shows the conditions in the prison. It also honors those who fought the regime, bringing to light their resistance efforts.

Salazar worked to suppress the Republican resistance that was fighting the oppressive regime in Spain.

For two decades after World War II ended in 1945, Salazar remained in firm control of Portugal until he fell ill in 1968. Marcello Caetano, who had worked with Salazar since the establishment of the New State, took over as leader. But the political and economic system of the New State remained the same.

The Carnation Revolution

Even as Salazar was keeping tight control over Portugal, the Portuguese colonies were in turmoil. Starting in the 1960s, the people living under Portuguese rule in Angola, Mozambique, Guinea-Bissau, India, and elsewhere began to revolt. Portugal's response was to send more and more soldiers overseas, to keep the colonies under their control. But it was a lost cause. The people wanted to rule themselves and make their own decisions. Many Portuguese soldiers did not want to die fighting to keep people from gaining their freedom. And Portuguese civilians did not want to see more of their money thrown away fighting endless colonial wars. Ending the wars would mean the independence of the colonies.

Some military officers began planning a coup to overthrow the New State and end the wars. The officers played songs on the radio to send signals. At 10:55 p.m. on April 24, 1974, a song called "E Depois do Adeus" ("And After the Farewell") sung by Paulo de Carvalho was aired. This song alerted the rebels to be ready. Then, shortly after midnight a song called "Grândola, Vila Morena" was played. It was by Zeca Afonso, a folk musician who was banned from the radio because of the political content of his songs. This song signaled to troops around the country to take up positions at key points. The revolution had begun.

The following morning, many Portuguese took to the streets in support of the military coup. In Lisbon, some soldiers put red carnations into the barrels of their guns, a signal that this would be a peaceful revolution. And it was. The dictatorial New State regime was ousted in the Carnation Revolution without a shot being fired.

The End of the Colonial Era

In 1975, Portugal's colonies gained independence, one after the other. The end of the colonial era was messy, however. Many of the Portuguese who had been running the government offices and ministries that kept the colonies functioning fled, many fearing the people they had been ruling. They made hasty

Portuguese fill the streets of Lisbon a few days after the Carnation Revolution.

departures by boat and plane back to Portugal. At the same time, many Angolans fled as well, not seeing a place for themselves in the newly independent nation. In all, more than half a million people left the former colonies for Portugal.

Dramatic Changes

In 1976, a new constitution was adopted, and Portugal held its first democratic legislative elections in half a century. Mário

Soares of the Socialist Party became the new prime minister. But the nation faced huge economic problems, including high unemployment and spiraling inflation, and Soares soon lost power. Control of the government changed hands several times in the following years as the economy continued to be unstable.

In 1986, Portugal joined the European Economic Community, now called the European Union (EU), an organization with the aim of integrating and improving the economy of its member nations. People, money, and goods move freely between the nations of the EU.

Portugal is the poorest nation in western Europe. After

joining the EU, the outlook for its economy changed overnight. Suddenly, there was massive investment in roads and buildings with an influx of funds from the EU. At the same time, many corporations and government officials saw an opportunity to line their own pockets. Spending for luxury items was so out of control that the EU ordered Portugal to cut its budget. In 1999, Portugal was one of eleven European nations that began using a common currency, the euro. These changes helped improve Portugal's economy.

Great investments were made in Portugal in the 1990s. Lisbon's new Orient Railway Station opened in 1998.

Recent Times

Despite these positive changes, Portugal was amassing enormous debt. By 2010, the country was in a financial crisis and had to take a huge loan from global banks to continue running its basic services. The government was forced to raise taxes, cut salaries for government employees, and reduce government benefits for people in need. People took to the streets to protest these austerity measures.

University students protest cuts to education in 2012.

In 2015, the government of Portugal decided to end its austerity program, despite complaints from the organizations to which it owed money. The Portuguese government raised wages for public employees and improved benefits. These changes produced quick results. People began spending more money, foreign businesses increased investment in Portugal, and exports increased. The economy is continuing to grow, and people are looking to the future with great optimism.

Travelers rush through the busy São Bento Railway Station in Porto. The station is famed for its tile murals that illustrate the history of the nation.

CHAPTER 5

Governing
the Republic

PORTUGAL IS A REPUBLIC, A FORM OF GOVERNMENT where the power is held by the people. They elect officials to represent them in their interests. Portugal has had several constitutions over the years. The current one was adopted in 1976, after the end of the dictatorship of António de Oliveira Salazar. It has been amended, or changed, twice since then to reflect the nation's changing political and economic ideas.

Opposite: **The Assembly of the Republic meets in São Bento Palace in Lisbon.**

The Executive Branch

Governments are divided into three different parts, or branches: executive, legislative, and judicial. The executive branch is in charge of enforcing the laws and carrying out the work of the government. In Portugal, the head of state is the president, who is elected by the people to a five-year term. The president may serve two consecutive terms. The

Portugal's National Government

Executive Branch
President
Prime Minister
Council of Ministers

Legislative Branch
Assembly of the Republic
(230 members)

Judicial Branch
Constitutional Court
Supreme Court
Court of Appeal
District Courts

president is the symbolic leader of the country and the commander in chief of the armed forces.

The head of the government is the prime minister. He or she is the leader of the party or group of parties that holds the most seats in the parliament. The prime minister is responsible for implementing policy. He or she is aided by a Council of Ministers. Each minister oversees a different aspect of government or policy. There are ministers of justice, finance, education, culture, and more.

The Legislative Branch

The legislative branch of government is the parliament, which is called the Assembly of the Republic. It has 230 mem-

António Guterres has worked in politics and diplomacy since he was in his mid-twenties.

Serving the World

In 2017, António Guterres became the secretary-general of the United Nations, an international organization devoted to promoting cooperation and settling disputes among countries. That makes him the world's top diplomat.

Guterres began his political career as a member of the Assembly of the Republic when he was only a few years out of college. After nearly two decades in the assembly, he became prime minister in 1995.

As prime minister, he was instrumental in changing how Portugal dealt with drug addiction. Under his leadership, Portugal decriminalized the use of drugs, treating it as a health issue rather than a crime. As a result of these changes, overall drug use declined and the number of people dying from overdoses dropped dramatically.

Later, Guterres served as the United Nations High Commissioner for Refugees, an organization that works to help people who have been forced from their homes by war or other dangers. His efforts came during a period in which more people were displaced from their homelands than at any time in history. After ten years of serving as the High Commissioner for Refugees, he was selected to be secretary-general, the head of the entire United Nations.

bers who are elected to four-year terms. The country is divided into eighteen districts. The number of representatives each district elects varies depending on the population of the district. Lisbon, the most populous district, is allotted forty-seven members of parliament. Portalegre, in east-central Portugal,

**Socialist Party leader
António Costa attends a
political rally in Lisbon
shortly before becoming
prime minister.**

gets two. The Azores and Madeira also send members to parliament. In addition, Portuguese living elsewhere in Europe and in the rest of the world also vote for representatives. Each group elects two members of the assembly.

The two major political parties in Portugal are the Socialist Party, which is more liberal, and the Social Democratic Party, which is more conservative. There are also many smaller parties, some of which have enough support that they win seats in the assembly. As a result, one single party does not usually hold a majority of the seats, and parties must work together in a coalition to form a government. For example, in 2015 the Socialist Party won 86 seats, but combined with four small parties, they had more than half the seats, allowing them to govern the country. If members of the assembly become dissatisfied with the direction of the government, they can hold a vote of no confidence. If the vote fails, the prime minister is dismissed and new elections are held.

The National Anthem

Portugal's national anthem, "A Portuguesa" ("The Portuguese"), was written in 1890. It was used as a rallying cry for people who wanted to end the monarchy and establish a more democratic form of government. When Portugal became a republic in 1910, the song was adopted as the national anthem. The music is by Alfredo Keil and the words were written by Henrique Lopes de Mendonça.

Portuguese lyrics

Heróis do mar, nobre povo,
Naçao valente, imortal,
Levantai hoje de novo
O esplendor de Portugal
Entre as brumas da memória.
Ó Pátria sente-se a voz
Dos teus egrégios avós
Que há-de guiar-te à vitória.

Às armas! Às armas!
Sobre a terra, sobre o mar!
Às armas! Às armas!
Pela Pátria lutar!
Contra os canhões marchar, marchar!

English translation

Heroes of the sea, noble race,
Valiant and immortal nation,
Rise up once again
The splendor of Portugal.
Out of the mists of memory,
Oh Homeland, we hear the voices
Of your great forefathers
That shall lead you on to victory!

To arms, to arms
On land and sea!
To arms, to arms
To fight for our Homeland!
To march against the enemy guns!

The Changing of the Guard ceremony in front of Belém Palace, the home of the president

The National Flag

The Portuguese flag features two broad sections of color with a coat of arms where the colors meet. The smaller portion is bright green and the larger portion is vivid red. The coat of arms features a shield on a gold armillary sphere, a model that shows the circles around the earth, such as the equator. The sphere symbolizes Portugal's history of exploration.

Portugal's flag was adopted in 1911, a year after the nation became a republic.

The Judicial Branch

The judicial branch of government consists of the court system. Most cases begin in the district courts. Rulings in district courts can be reviewed in a court of appeal. The highest court in the land is the Supreme Court. It is the highest court to hear appeals, or review, cases from lower courts. It also tries high government officials.

Portugal has a separate Constitutional Court. It evaluates whether laws or rules violate the constitution.

Regional and Local Government

Two parts of Portugal are known as autonomous regions: the Azores and Madeira. This means they have greater self-government than other parts of the country. Each has its own president, cabinet, and legislature.

The rest of the country is divided into eighteen districts, each with an appointed governor. These districts are divided into municipalities and parishes.

A Look at the Capital

About half a million people live within the city limits of Lisbon, Portugal's capital. The greater metropolitan area has a population of about 2.8 million.

Lisbon is a modern city with a long history. The city was a thriving metropolis when a massive earthquake struck in 1755, destroying almost all of the city's buildings. When Lisbon was rebuilt, city planners created a highly organized urban plan. Lisbon's streets range from narrow lanes, with shops and homes crowded together, to wide boulevards. The wide avenues were created during the time of Portugal's great seafaring expeditions. An aqueduct was built to bring water to the citizens.

Modern Lisbon is built on seven hills. The oldest part of the city is centered on an area

Trams carry people through Lisbon's narrow streets.

called the Baixa. Some of the oldest Portuguese architecture is found here, including the Castle of St. George, which dates to the time of the Moors. Nearby is the Alfama district, an old neighborhood of narrow streets and Moorish architecture that survived the earthquake.

Monuments to the city's past are found close to the Tagus River. These include the Belém Tower, which was built as part of the city's defenses in the 1500s. Belém Palace, built in the same era, was once home to kings but is now home to the president of the republic. The Jerónimos Monastery also dates to the 1500s.

Today, Lisbon is a major financial center and the country's largest seaport. It is also the cultural heart of the nation. Major museums include the National Museum of Ancient Art, the Calouste Gulbenkian Museum, and the National Azulejo Museum. The University of Lisbon is the country's largest university.

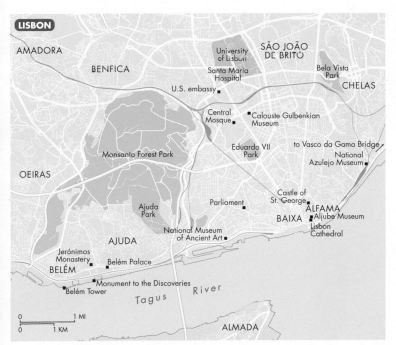

LISBON

AMADORA
BENFICA
SÃO JOÃO DE BRITO
University of Lisbon
Santa Maria Hospital
Bela Vista Park
CHELAS
U.S. embassy
Central Mosque
Calouste Gulbenkian Museum
Eduardo VII Park
to Vasco da Gama Bridge
National Azulejo Museum
Monsanto Forest Park
OEIRAS
Ajuda Park
Parliament
Castle of St. George
ALFAMA
BAIXA
Aljube Museum
Lisbon Cathedral
National Museum of Ancient Art
AJUDA
Jerónimos Monastery
Belém Palace
BELÉM
Monument to the Discoveries
Belém Tower
Tagus River
ALMADA
0   1 MI
0   1 KM

CHAPTER 6

Portugal at Work

PORTUGAL HAS A DIVERSE ECONOMY THAT BENEFITS from its geographic location and its well-educated workforce. More and more, Portugal is becoming the home of modern technology companies. Most younger Portuguese are fluent in English, which is appealing to international companies.

When Portugal joined the European Union in 1986, the nation began to change its economy. Though the transition to a more modern economy was difficult, most people welcomed the changes. Now, Portugal proudly takes its place as one of the most progressive and open countries among its neighbors.

Opposite: **In the Douro Valley, farmers cut terraced fields into the hillsides to grow grapevines. People in the region have been turning grapes into wine for more than two thousand years.**

Agriculture

Agriculture accounts for only a small amount of Portugal's economy. Much of the land, however, is devoted to farms,

Cork trees and sunflowers grow well in dry areas where little rain falls.

Adjusting to a Changing Climate

The global climate is changing. Human activity such as burning coal and driving cars sends pollutants into the air, which trap heat near the earth. In some parts of the world, climate change has caused more severe storms. In Portugal, it has caused scorching heat and less rainfall, forcing many people to change the way they earn a living.

Successful farming is dependent on water and the right amount of sunshine. In most regions of Portugal, farmers water their crops through irrigation. The water often comes from water diverted by dams built on the Tagus River. While the irrigation from the river helps farmers, the amount of water available varies depending upon rainfall, and Portugal has experienced drier conditions than usual in recent years. In 2017, the lakes created by the country's dams were at their lowest levels in thirty years. Some farmers have had to change the type of crops they grow. Cereals such as corn and rice require a lot of water, so cereal production has been decreasing.

orchards, and vineyards. One of the nation's major agricultural areas is the Alentejo region, which stretches across much of southern Portugal. Wheat, corn, and barley are grown in this region.

Many fruits are grown in Portugal, including olives, oranges, cherries, and pears. Grapes cover the hillsides in the Douro Valley. The grapes are used to make wine, one of the nation's leading exports. Recent wildfires have devastated some of the grape-growing regions. The 2017 wildfires burned roughly 20 percent of the grape farmlands. It is feared that some of the vineyards will not recover.

What Portugal Grows, Makes, and Mines

Agriculture (2016)

Tomatoes	1,693,860 metric tons
Grapes	773,904 metric tons
Olives	617,610 metric tons

Manufacturing (2016, value of exports)

Paper goods	$2.85 billion
Vehicle parts	$2.29 billion
Refined oil	$2.18 billion

Mining

Copper (2014)	75,433 metric tons
Zinc (2014)	67,384 metric tons
Tungsten (2017)	680 metric tons

Fishing and Forestry

With its long coastline, fishing has always been important in Portugal. Commercial fishers in large boats work the deep waters offshore, staying at sea for days and even weeks. Among the fish they catch are tuna, sardines, mackerel, and cod.

Small boats with a few fishers, often members of one family, go out early in the morning, work all day, and then bring their catch in to sell on the beach at the end of the day. They go after octopus and fish such as hake, sardines, and conger. The work is hard and depends on natural conditions far beyond the fishers' control. These workers make up more than 80 percent of the Portuguese engaged in fishing, but they bring in only 8 percent of the fish caught in the waters around Portugal.

Portugal is a major producer of cork, producing about half the cork in the world. Cork trees grow across much of southern Portugal. Other areas are populated with eucalyptus or pine. Many of these trees are used to make paper.

Manufacturing and Mining

Industry makes up about 22 percent of the economy. A wide variety of goods are produced in Portugal. Grapes are turned into wine and olives into olive oil. Factories turn out cars and car parts, plastics, machinery, and chemicals. There are companies that produce leather shoes, textiles, and ceramics. Others manufacture furniture. About a quarter of Portuguese workers are employed in industry.

Portugal has a small but important mining industry. It is one of Europe's largest producers of copper. Other important minerals unearthed in Portugal include tungsten, tin, and uranium.

Services

Service industries make up by far the largest part of the Portuguese economy. Service industries include a wide variety of jobs. People who work in medicine,

RESOURCES

KEY

	Forest
	Pasture
	Cropland
	Cropland and pasture
	Mediterranean crops
Cu	Copper
Dm	Diamond
Fe	Iron
⚒	Oil
Pb	Lead
Sn	Tin
U	Uranium
W	Tungsten
Zn	Zinc

SPAIN

Workers lay decorative cobblestones at a site in the Azores. Construction has boomed in Portugal in recent years.

education, trade, and banking are all employed in service industries.

Tourism is a major service industry. Millions of people travel to Portugal each year to enjoy the sunny beaches and historic cities. Many Portuguese work in hotels, restaurants, and other businesses that serve tourists.

A booming technology park with offices of more than one hundred companies has been built in Oeiras, on the outskirts of Lisbon. Oeiras has quickly become the technology headquarters of Portugal. It has attracted many international companies, including Canon, Dell, Cisco, Intel, Epson, Google, and Samsung.

Portugal's ability to produce technology workers and

engineers is demonstrated at a conference called the Web Summit, which the country has hosted for three years. This conference attracts between fifty and sixty thousand participants each year. The three-day event features hundreds of speakers from all areas of industry and entertainment. The event is attended by some of the most innovative people in the world, many of whom want to start new technology-related businesses that will drive innovation and create jobs.

Vacationers fill a beach in southern Portugal. In 2017, 12.7 million foreign tourists traveled to Portugal, nearly double the number from a decade earlier.

Transportation

Portugal has a modern transportation system. Roads and railroads connect cities with Portugal, and the national airline, TAP, connects Portugal to the rest of the world. The airline has its headquarters in Lisbon. It operates about 2,500 flights a week, flying to destinations in thirty-four countries.

Portugal's ports have been expanded in recent years, so they can accommodate a growing number of cargo ships and cruise ships.

The Vasco da Gama Bridge, which spans the Tagus River in Lisbon, is the longest bridge entirely within Europe.

Money Facts

Until recently, each nation in Europe used its own type of currency. The money in Portugal was called the escudo. In 1999, eleven European countries began using a brand-new currency called the euro, which is divided into one hundred cents. At first euros were used only in electronic forms such as money transfers, but then in 2002 physical bills and coins were introduced.

To make the change, people in Portugal and other European countries exchanged their old banknotes for the new currency. Billions of banknotes and coins were taken out of circulation and replaced with the new money. Every time a person bought something with escudos, the change would be given in euros. ATM machines dispensed euros instead of escudos. In this way, the transition was smooth.

Euro bills are issued in values of 5, 10, 20, 50, 100, 200, and 500 euros. Each denomination of euro is a different color and size, with the smallest denomination being the smallest size note. Euro notes look the same in all the countries that use them. They feature windows or gateways on the front and bridges on the back. In order to make the notes acceptable to people in many different countries, the designs depict periods of architecture rather than specific sites.

Euro coins are issued in eight values: 1, 2, 5, 10, 20, and 50 cents, and 1 and 2 euros. Each country that uses euros makes its own coins. The coins have a map of Europe on one side and symbols that relate to the country on the other. In Portugal, the coins feature various versions of the royal seal and old Portuguese castles.

In 2018, 1 euro equaled $1.14, and $1.00 equaled 0.87 euros.

CHAPTER 7

Home and School

PORTUGAL IS HOME TO ABOUT TEN MILLION PEOPLE. Portugal's population has declined in recent years, as people have moved to other parts of the European Union or the world for work. In addition, families have gotten smaller, and Portugal now has one of the lowest birth rates in the world.

Opposite: **In the old part of Porto, red-roofed buildings are crowded together on narrow streets.**

Cities, Suburbs, and Villages

About two-thirds of the people in Portugal live in urban areas, mostly along the coast midway down the country. The old parts of cities such as Lisbon and Porto are filled with historic buildings and narrow streets. The majority of the people, however, live in the suburbs on the outskirts of the cities. In recent years, many young people and foreigners have been moving into the cities' old neighborhoods. This is causing

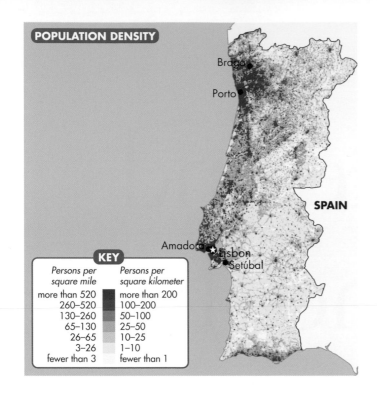

Braga

Porto

SPAIN

Amadora
Lisbon
Setúbal

KEY

Persons per square mile	Persons per square kilometer
more than 520	more than 200
260–520	100–200
130–260	50–100
65–130	25–50
26–65	10–25
3–26	1–10
fewer than 3	fewer than 1

rents to rise dramatically, forcing many long-time residents of these neighborhoods out of their homes.

Over the last few decades, many rural areas have been losing population. As farming has declined, people have moved to the cities or out of the country entirely. As a result, many villages have been completely abandoned.

The People of Portugal

Lisbon is the most cosmopolitan city in Portugal. Most people who live there are of Mediterranean descent, but an increasing number are immigrants from other parts of the world. In the twentieth century, many immigrants in Portugal were from former colonies, especially Cabo Verde. More recently, migrants have been coming from other former colonies such as Angola and Brazil as well as from eastern European countries such as Ukraine and Romania.

Language

Language is one of the most important ways in which people identify themselves culturally, and the Portuguese people take tremendous pride in their language. With its small population, few people spoke Portuguese until explorers set out in the 1400s, and the era of colonization began. As the Portuguese established colonies around the world, use of the language

**Population of
Major Cities
(2018 est.)**

Lisbon	517,802
Porto	249,633
Amadora	178,858
Braga	121,394
Setúbal	117,110

spread. Today, it is a main or official language in the South American nation of Brazil as well in the African nations of Cabo Verde, Guinea-Bissau, Mozambique, Angola, and São Tomé and Príncipe. It is still spoken in other former Portuguese colonies, including Goa in India, Macau in China, and the Southeast Asian nation of East Timor. It is the seventh most spoken language in the world, with about 223 million native speakers. The vast majority of them are in Brazil.

Portuguese and Brazilians speak the language in slightly different ways. While the two different groups can understand each other, Portuguese speak more quickly than Brazilians, and they don't pronounce the words as clearly. Other

Ethnicity

Portuguese 95%

Other (including African, Brazilian, and Chinese) 5%

Chinese Portuguese perform at a Chinese New Year celebration.

A sign in Madeira warns of a dangerous cliff. In areas where many tourists visit, some signs are translated into English.

differences arise as new words are created, especially in the world of technology. Sometimes an English word is used instead of a Portuguese word.

Portugal has one of the highest literacy rates in the world. Being able to read and write one's own language is more than a matter of pride. It means that people can understand the laws that govern them and the contracts they sign. They can read the labels on the foods and other products they buy. It means they can make decisions based on facts.

Portuguese children are also expected to learn other languages. Instruction in English is now introduced in primary school. This helps young people find work in many places in the world.

School Days

In Portugal, education is free for all children. Public education is an important ingredient in making sure

Say It in Portuguese

Olá	Hello
Adeus	Good-bye
Sim	Yes
Não	No
Faz favor	Please
Obrigado	Thank you
Bom dia	Good morning
Grande	Big
Pequeno	Small

An elderly man reads a newspaper in Lisbon. Portugal's literacy rate increased from roughly 80 to 95 percent between 1981 and 2011.

that all children, whatever their parents' income level or background, get a good education. The quality of education is high, so most people go to public schools, but there are some private schools, mostly in Lisbon and Porto.

Children are required to attend school from age six to eighteen. The first nine years of school, everyone studies the same subjects, such as math, science, history, and music. They also learn English as well as a second foreign language.

The last three years of school, students move on different tracks. Students who want to go to university focus on

academic classes. Other students follow an art-oriented curriculum. Young people who want to go straight into work after completing school follow a technology or work program. They study subjects such as computer programming or electronics.

In Portugal, the school schedule is similar to that in the United States. The school year starts in September and runs through June, with a long summer break. Young children typically go to school from about 9 a.m. to 3:30 p.m. The school day for older children is a bit longer.

Portugal has more than a dozen public universities and several private universities. The largest is the University of Porto, which serves about twenty-eight thousand students. The University of Coimbra is one of the oldest universities in the world. It was originally established in 1290 in Lisbon. In 1537, the school was moved north, to the city of Coimbra.

Every May in Portugal, university students organize Queima das Fitas ("ribbon burning") festivities celebrating the coming end of the school year. At a parade in Porto, students carry hats and canes in the color of their school within the university. Yellow is for students in the medical college.

Home and School **91**

CHAPTER 8

A Matter of Faith

LTHOUGH PORTUGAL DOES NOT HAVE AN OFFICIAL religion, it has a strong connection to the Roman Catholic faith. More than 80 percent of the people identify as Catholic, although most do not actively practice the faith. Many Portuguese who do not go to Mass regularly may still get married in a church and have their children baptized.

Opposite: **For many religious festivals, Portuguese hold processions, carrying a statue through town.**

Other Religions

About 3 percent of the people follow other Christian religions. These include Anglicanism, Methodism, Pentecostalism, and Jehovah's Witness.

About fifty thousand Portuguese are Muslims. Many of them are immigrants from former Portuguese colonies. The Central Mosque of Lisbon is the nation's largest mosque.

Religious Practice	
Roman Catholic	81%
No religion	7%
Protestant	3%
Other	9%

Portugal is also home to an estimated ten thousand Buddhists, mainly from the former colony of Macau, and about seven thousand Hindus. There are also an estimated one thousand Jewish people in the country.

Religious Sites

In Portugal, people in the northern part of the country have traditionally been more religiously observant than those who live in the south. But it is central Portugal that is home to many magnificent churches and shrines. The Church of Saint Francis in Porto is renowned for its ornate interior, much of it

Portuguese president Marcelo Rebelo de Sousa (right) attends a celebration honoring the Muslim community in Lisbon.

Alcobaça Monastery was founded by King Afonso Henriques.

The Alcobaça Monastery

North of the Tagus River is the Alcobaça Monastery, the largest church in Portugal. Work was begun on this magnificent complex of buildings in 1153, and the first building was completed in 1223. These were the first Gothic buildings in Portugal. Gothic architecture features soaring, pointed arches and extensive use of stained glass. Construction continued through the centuries, and the tombs of many Portuguese monarchs are found here.

covered in gold. The eighteenth-century Carmo Church has a wall covered with azulejo tiles that depict the founding of the church. One of the most notable churches in Braga, the Church of Bom Jesus do Monte, sits on a hilltop. The faithful climb 577 steps up a zigzagging staircase to reach it. Although

Jacinta, Francisco, and Lucia told their families they saw a vision while they were herding sheep.

Some believers approach the shrine at Fátima on their knees.

Place of Pilgrimage

In 1917, three children in Fátima, in central Portugal, claimed they saw a vision they believed was the Virgin Mary, the mother of Jesus. According to the legend, the vision reappeared one day every month after that, for several months. The children said that the vision had told them that there would be a major miracle in October. An estimated seventy thousand people gathered at Fátima on October 13. People claim that the sun emitted multicolored lights and careened around the sky. This event became known as the Miracle of the Sun.

The story of this site has made the small town of Fátima into one of the most important places in the world for many Catholics. Through the years, millions of people have made a religious journey, or pilgrimage, to Fátima. They feel blessed by being where the children said they saw the vision. Many of the pilgrims are sick or disabled and come to Fátima to pray for miracle cures.

In 1967, Pope Paul VI, the leader of the Roman Catholic Church, visited Fátima on the fiftieth anniversary of the first vision, and in 2000, Pope John Paul II visited Fátima. Then, in 2017, on the one-hundredth anniversary of the original vision, Pope Francis canonized two of the children, officially making them saints, holy people in the eyes of the Church.

the current church dates to the 1700s, this hill has held chapels since the 1300s.

Feasts and Festivals

In Portugal, the year is punctuated by religious festivals. Many of the most colorful festivals take place in the north and in towns not far from Lisbon. Towns often celebrate the life of a particular saint associated with it, so religious observances vary from one region to another.

Porto's Church of Saint Francis was built in a simple Gothic style in the 1300s and 1400s. In the 1700s, much of the interior was covered in gold decoration. This ornate style is called Baroque.

During the week leading up to Easter, people in Monsanto, a town in east-central Portugal, dress in traditional clothing and take part in rituals recreating the story of Jesus's life.

Holy Week, which ends with Easter Sunday, is the most important religious festival of the year. In the north, Palm Sunday, a week before Easter, is marked by church members walking through the streets carrying palms. This is meant to symbolize Christ's entrance into Jerusalem. Lent, the forty days preceding Easter, is a solemn time, when many Catholics do without some of the things they particularly enjoy. For many, this means not eating meat or some other food.

For Carnival in northern Portugal, some people dress as rowdy troublemakers called *caretos*. The tradition of caretos dates back to before the beginning of Christianity.

Carnival

For devout Catholics, the forty-day period before Easter known as Lent is a serious time. In many parts of the world, there is a tradition of having a great celebration, a last moment of revelry, immediately before Lent. This celebration is known as Carnival.

Centuries ago, many Carnival celebrants wore masks as a way to hide their identities while they were behaving in a particularly wild way. In Portugal, Carnival celebrations combine traditional costumes along with street dancing.

One of the most popular Carnivals in Portugal takes place in the city of Torres Vedras, about 30 miles (50 km) north of Lisbon. This event features a grand parade with elaborate floats. These floats often carry giant, mocking puppets of well-known political figures. Participants spend months preparing for this festival.

CHAPTER 9

Creative Life

SPORTS, THEATER, ART, TV, AND SINGING ARE ALL parts of life in Portugal. Like most Europeans, Portuguese are passionate about soccer. The whole nation comes to a standstill when their top player, Cristiano Ronaldo, is on the field for the national team. Many of the favorite cultural activities in Portugal are similar to those in the United States, except the language is different. Popular television programs include a quiz show that challenges contestants with questions in different categories. It's like a combination of *Jeopardy!* and *Who Wants to Be a Millionaire.*

Portuguese telenovelas, similar to American soap operas, have many devoted followers. They usually feature dramatic situations involving several generations of a family with a lot of romance, misunderstandings, and complicated stories.

Portuguese-language television also offers talk shows, news

Opposite: **Street artists Vhils and Pixel Pancho collaborated on this artwork in Lisbon. Portugal is renowned for its street art.**

The Portuguese guitar often accompanies fado songs. The round guitar has twelve strings, which are played by plucking.

shows, and sports broadcasts. There are crime shows, dramas, musical shows, shows for children, and medical dramas, all the same types of shows familiar to American viewers.

Music

Portugal is famed for its unique singing style called fado. The minute the first notes of a traditional fado song are heard, the listener knows to prepare for a haunting, sweet, and sad song. The word *fado* means "fate" or "destiny." Fado music is said to express a unique Portuguese feeling called *saudade*, meaning "longing," that something has been lost. Fado has been around since the early 1800s, originating in the bars and cafés of Lisbon. While fado is a traditional type of music, it has been taken up by a new generation of younger artists.

Portugal's most famous *fadista*, a singer of fado, was Amália Rodrigues. Her passionate singing style helped popularize fado around the world. Among the young fadistas are Ana Moura and Mariza. Ana Moura combines the feeling of fado with modern pop music. One of her albums, *Desfado*, was among the top-selling albums in Portugal for more than two years. Mariza was born in what is now Mozambique during the colonial period and came to Portugal as a child. She is renowned internationally.

Many other kinds of music are also popular in Portugal. People listen to folk music and classical, hip-hop and rock. The biggest singing competition in all of Europe is called Eurovision. The event, which features one contestant per

Although she died in 1999, Amália Rodrigues remains the best-selling Portuguese singer of all time.

Calouste Gulbenkian collected thousands of pieces of art during his lifetime. Many of these are now on display.

The Gulbenkian Museum

The most prominent art center in Lisbon is the Calouste Gulbenkian Museum. Gulbenkian was a businessperson who grew wealthy working in the oil industry. Over his life, as he traveled the globe, he amassed one of the world's greatest art collections.

The unique collection includes both ancient and contemporary art. There are works from ancient Greece and Rome and from eighteenth-century France. There are eighteenth-century statues and rare illuminated manuscripts.

Gulbenkian was born in what is now Istanbul, Turkey, and held British citizenship, but he spent his last few years living in Lisbon. It was there that he decided to establish a museum where much of his art would be displayed. He died in 1955, and the museum opened in 1969.

country, is televised and draws hundreds of millions of viewers. In 2017, Portuguese singer Salvador Sobral won top honors. Sobral performed a song written by his sister, Luísa Sobral, one of the most important young songwriters and singers in Portugal.

Art

Portugal has a rich history in the visual arts. Nuno Gonçalves was a master painter from the 1400s. He is most famous for the Saint Vincent Panels, a series of paintings that depict different segments of society. In the late 1700s, sculptor Joaquim Machado de Castro became prominent. His classical works include a powerful sculpture of King Joseph I on horseback that sits high on a pedestal in Commerce Square in Lisbon. The twentieth century saw the emergence of modernism. One of the finest Portuguese artists of this era was abstract painter Maria Helena Vieira da Silva.

More recently, Portuguese artists have been exploring a wide range of subjects and styles. Painter and sculptor Vasco Araújo is inspired by both Portugal's colonial history and natural objects such as plants. Hazul Luzah is a graffiti artist who works on the streets of Porto. His work, in blue and white, captures lively interpretations of nature. It also bears a close relationship to the most

Nuno Gonçalves painted the Saint Vincent Panels in the 1400s. They disappeared after Lisbon's earthquake in 1775 and were not rediscovered until 1882.

traditional of all Portuguese arts, tiles called azulejos.

Another Portuguese artist, Alexandre Farto, who works under the name Vhils, is one of the world's top street artists. He has developed entirely new styles, digging through years of posters and plaster to etch into the cement or brick below.

Literature

Portugal is proud of its literary history. A giant among Portuguese writers is Luís de Camões, a poet who was born nearly five hundred years ago. Although Portugal has many contemporary poets at work today, the nation still celebrates

Maria Helena Vieira da Silva at work on a painting. She was known for her intricate compositions.

A man walks by azulejo tiles on a church in Porto.

Azulejos

In some ways, azulejos can be called the original street art because they can be seen on the outer walls of buildings all around Portugal. These ceramic tiles, often in blue and white, are beautiful as well as sturdy. They are seen on churches, homes, palaces, and such well-known sites as the São Bento Railway Station, the Buçaco Palace, and many stops in the Lisbon subway system. The tiles often depict scenes from Portuguese history. The National Azulejo Museum in Lisbon shows how tiles developed in Portugal through the centuries.

Camões, its best-known literary figure. As a young man, he became a soldier and traveled widely throughout areas of India ruled by Portugal, gathering impressions for the long poem he would write on his return. Titled "Os Lusíadas" ("The Lusitanians"), the poem celebrates Portugal's history. Camões used the voyage of the Portuguese explorer Vasco da Gama as

Luís de Camões is buried in the Jerónimos Monastery in Lisbon.

a way of describing the history of the Portuguese. The poem is an epic celebration of Portuguese culture. The day Camões died, June 10, is a national holiday called the Day of Portugal, Camões, and the Portuguese Communities.

Another celebrated Portuguese poet is Fernando Pessoa. Writing in the early twentieth century, he brought a modern, innovative quality to Portuguese literature. Pessoa wrote under many different names, each with a distinct style, personality, and philosophy. In some cases, he wrote criticism of the work of one of his personas while writing under another name. People did not know that these many writers were the same person until after he died.

Portugal's most celebrated writer is José Saramago, who won the Nobel Prize in Literature, the world's most prestigious literary prize, in 1998. While Saramago was growing up, there was no hint that he would become a world-renowned writer. His family was too poor to keep him in school. Instead, he studied to become a mechanic. His own literary education took place in a public library in Lisbon, where he studied at night. He worked as a translator, turning foreign authors' works into Portuguese. Saramago was in his fifties by the time he began writing the novels that would bring him acclaim. His work had a distinctive style, with long sentences and

José Saramago was the first Portuguese writer to win the Nobel Prize in Literature.

little punctuation. In his novels, he sometimes used fantastical elements as a way to comment on the problems of the real world. Saramago's novels upset the government because of their social and political content, and when one of his books was censored, he left Portugal to live in the Canary Islands, off the west coast of Africa. He died there in 2010.

Sports

The most popular sport in Portugal is soccer. Cristiano Ronaldo, one of the game's greatest players, was born on the island of Madeira. Portuguese fill stadiums to watch Premiere

Children play soccer on the street in Lisbon.

League teams play. The three top teams are Benefica and Sporting, both based in Lisbon, and Porto. When the national team competes against teams from other nations, everyone is glued to the TV. One of the national team's greatest triumphs was winning the European championship in 2016. Other sports popular in Portugal include basketball, rugby, and cycling.

Portugal has sent a team to the summer Olympics every four years since 1912. In 1952, Portugal began competing in the winter Olympics as well. All of Portugal's medals have been won during the summer events. Many of Portugal's greatest Olympic athletes have been runners. Carlos Lopes was the first person from Portugal to win an Olympic gold medal. He triumphed in the marathon, a grueling 26-mile (42 km) road race, in 1984. Four years later, Rosa Mota became the first Portuguese woman to

Fans show their enthusiasm for the Portuguese national soccer team during a match against Spain.

Horses and Bulls

Portugal has a long tradition of a type of horse riding known as dressage. In this sport, riders and horses perform as a unit, with the rider guiding the horse through intricate movements. The horse sometimes seems to be dancing as it prances around in a very disciplined way. In Portugal in the late 1700s, the Marquês de Marialva, who was known as the King's Master of the Horse, was famous for performing the most difficult techniques of the sport.

The ability to control the horse's movements in such a precise way led to the use of horses in the bullfighting ring. Unlike in neighboring Spain, the bull is never killed in Portuguese bullfighting. Instead, the event shows the rider's skills and the horse's abilities as they move the bull around the ring.

Many Portuguese dressage riders and bullfighters use a horse breed called the Lusitano. This Portuguese breed is famed for being intelligent, gentle, and agile.

win Olympic gold, also in the marathon. Portuguese athletes have also taken home medals in sports such as judo, sailing, and horse riding, or equestrianism.

Many Portuguese and visitors to the country love water sports. They enjoy sailing, kayaking, scuba diving, and surfing. Around the world, there are a few places where enormous waves attract the best and bravest surfers. The village of Nazaré on Portugal's central coast is one of these dramatic sites. The monstrous waves there form because the underwater Nazaré Canyon channels the water. The sea curls up into walls of water as much as 100 feet (30 m) high, challenging the world's best surfers.

A surfer races down a towering wave at Nazaré.

CHAPTER 10

Tradition and Change

I N RECENT DECADES, PORTUGAL HAS MOVED RAPIDLY into the modern world. Like many people from other countries, Portuguese go to work in offices, travel in airplanes around the world, stream TV shows on their laptops, and use their phones to communicate with friends in other countries. At the same time, the Portuguese people have retained traditional ways and a sense of politeness and respect that has long been important in their culture. Children are expected to have good manners and to treat their elders with respect. Family life remains a crucial part of everyday life.

Opposite: **Elderly men walk up a hill in a town in Algarve. Nearly one in five Portuguese is older than sixty-five.**

Family Traditions

Ceremonies are an important part of life in Portugal. Traditional Catholic rituals such as baptism are practiced. Engagement and marriage ceremonies are similar to those in

Naming Newborns

In the United States, new parents can name their children anything they like. Many other countries, including Portugal, have strict rules or laws about what babies can be named.

In Portugal, naming laws require that given names must be traditionally Portuguese unless one of the parents is foreign. Even then, the name must use the Portuguese spelling. So, for example, a baby could be named Kévim but not Kevin. In addition, the gender of the baby must be clear from the name. There are no names like Taylor, which are common for both boys and girls. Nor can a child's official name be a nickname or shortened version of a name. A newborn can be named Alexandre, but not Alex.

the United States. In many ways, funeral traditions are also similar to those in other countries, but in some places, old rituals endure. In villages, a death is announced by the ringing of church bells. In small towns and villages, the doors of the home of the deceased are sometimes left open to allow people to come in and take part in the grieving process.

Fun Time

Portuguese children play many of the same games as American children, including hopscotch and musical chairs, as well as games that are particular to Portugal.

A game called *bom barqueiro*, which means the "good boatman," is similar to London Bridge is falling down. In this game, two children are chosen to be the team leaders. They

Children sitting in a circle play a game in a square in Lisbon.

The Vasco da Gama Mall in Lisbon includes about 170 stores.

Going to the Mall

As Portugal has changed in recent decades, some activities of everyday life have changed as well. In the past, people would go to different shops to buy produce or meat, shoes or housewares. Today, city streets are still lined with small shops, but cities and towns now also have shopping malls. Many shopping malls around the country have more than one hundred stores, dozens of restaurants, movie theaters, supermarkets, medical clinics, pharmacies, and more. As in the United States, families like to spend time at malls because they offer so many choices.

pick team names and then face each other and form a bridge with their hands. The other children make a line and ask the boatman, in a song, to let them pass, running under the bridge. At the end of the song, the bridge comes down and one child is trapped. That child then decides which team to join and the game continues until all of the children have been trapped. A line is then drawn in the middle of a play area. The members of each team join hands in a long line and try to pull the other team over the line.

Food and Drink

Portugal's cuisine is based on the fresh ingredients that can be found all around the country: fish and shellfish from the sea; pork from pig farms; fresh vegetables and fruits from all around the country.

Fish is especially popular. Portuguese eat more fish on average than people in any other country in Europe. The variety of fish and seafood includes cod, sardines, hake, octopus, and crab. Sometimes the fish is grilled, fried, boiled, or steamed.

Codfish dry in the sun on the island of Madeira. Dried, salted cod, called bacalhau, is used in many Portuguese dishes. The Portuguese have been making this preserved fish since the 1400s because it could be brought on long ocean voyages.

White beans, sausage, and rice are common elements in Portuguese meals. Popular vegetables include tomatoes, potatoes, cabbage, and kale. Dishes are often flavored with garlic as well as spices such as pepper, cinnamon, and saffron.

In Portugal, breakfast is the simplest meal of the day. Many people have buttered toast and coffee. Some Portuguese also enjoy fruit or yogurt. Lunch and dinner are larger meals. They often include both a soup and a main course such as grilled fish or sausage. Desserts are typically custards, rice pudding, or pastries.

A huge variety of produce is available at Portuguese farmers markets.

Delicious Dessert

A perfect ending to a Portuguese meal is a dessert called *pastel de nata*, tarts of egg custard in a delicate, flaky pastry shell. The tarts are small, just a few bites each, and completely delicious. They were developed in Lisbon hundreds of years ago. According to a story, they were invented by monks and nuns who used egg whites to starch their religious robes. They began to use the leftover egg yolks to make the pastries.

Today, pastel de nata can be found in bakeries all over the country. People rush to get them while they are just out of the oven and still warm. In Lisbon, people enjoy a pastel de nata with a small cup of coffee called a *bica*, which is similar to Italian espresso.

Several dishes in Portugal can be called the national dish. One of the favorites is a stew known as *carne de porco à alentejana*. It combines ingredients that aren't usually found in the same dish: pork and clams. When a good cook stirs them together with the right spices, the result is delicious. Another food that stakes a claim as the national dish is a soup called

Changing Habits

American fast-food restaurants such as Pizza Hut and McDonald's are popular in Portugal's larger cities. These American chains adapt to the local foods and ways of eating in order to appeal to more customers. McDonald's includes Portuguese soups on the menu. These restaurants sometimes change their style to be more like typical Portuguese dining places. For example, some Pizza Hut restaurants use real silverware and tablecloths.

caldo verde, which translates to "green broth." It is made with kale or collard greens and potato, and often sausage or ham. Wine is an important part of many Portuguese meals. In fact, Portuguese drink more wine per person than people in almost any other country. Portugal has a long tradition of wine making. A sweet wine called port, made with grapes in the Douro Valley, is famous around the world. The port is aged in huge barrels in cellars in and around the city of Porto. Each year, millions of bottles of port are sold all around the world.

Festivals

The people of Portugal celebrate a huge variety of festivals. These events allow the local people to bring out their traditional costumes and jewelry, which are important parts of their cultural identity. Costumes in the Minho region in the northwest feature intricately embroidered scarves and aprons that display the designs of specific villages. Topping off the costumes is traditional Portuguese jewelry made of delicate

In the Algarve region, many dishes are cooked in a copper pot called a *cataplana*, which has a rounded lid that is clamped closed during cooking.

People carry flowers for an Easter procession in Algarve.

National Holidays

January 1	New Year's Day
March or April	Good Friday
March or April	Easter Sunday
April 25	Freedom Day
May 1	Labor Day
June 10	Day of Portugal, Camões, and the Portuguese Communities
May or June	Corpus Christi
August 15	Assumption Day
October 5	Republic Day
November 1	All Saints' Day
December 1	Restoration of Independence Day
December 8	Immaculate Conception
December 25	Christmas Day

gold filigree. Festivals combine religious observance, dancing, and feasting, and are often both solemn and joyful.

Many festivals honor the country's history and culture. The National Agriculture Fair in Santarém, in central Portugal,

Festival Costumes

Traditional Portuguese costumes are worn during many festivals. Both men and women wear elaborately embroidered outfits with designs that vary from village to village. Since they are made by hand, the costumes express the ideas and color choices of the maker.

The northern province of Minho is known for its colorful and finely made costumes. Sometimes the overall color of the costume expresses a mood. For example, red indicates happiness while blue and green show sadness. Elaborate rows of trim accent different areas of the costume.

There are also layers upon layers of fabric, giving the costume maker even more room for decoration and embroidery. As the women and men whirl around during a dance, they show off the many layers and colors of their work.

Gold jewelry is part of the traditional costume in Minho.

celebrates the country's agricultural production, and includes displays of folk dancing and bullfighting. The country's past is honored at the Medieval Fair in Santa Maria da Feira, in the northern part of the country. Visitors are transported back in time as artisans, soldiers, and others display their skills. A festival in Guimarães celebrates the nation's history with a torchlight procession, dancing, and a medieval parade. Many more Portuguese festivals have both religious and nonreligious elements. These are often the feast days of saints, so they include processions of religious statues through the streets before the

Drumming groups fill the streets during the feast of Saint John in Braga.

music, dancing, and other fun starts. Saint Anthony is honored in Lisbon's Alfama district. The fine June weather greets thousands of visitors who enjoy the singing, dancing, food and drink. Saint John's Day is celebrated in many cities. In Porto, people take part in new versions of ancient rituals, such as hitting each other with soft plastic hammers, before enjoying a spectacular fireworks display. In Braga, the streets are filled with drumming and other music.

Local foods and customs are marked by celebrations in seaside towns, including the Week of the Sea in the Azores. The largest festival in the Azores takes place in May and honors a statue known as Christ of the Miracles, which is believed to have miraculous qualities. The streets of the city of Ponta Delgada are covered with flowers as the statue is carried through town in a grand procession. For the rest of the day, people enjoy dancing, good food, and the company of friends and family.

The procession route through Ponta Delgada is covered with colorful flowers and dyed wood shavings for the feast honoring the Christ of the Miracles statue.

Timeline

Portuguese History

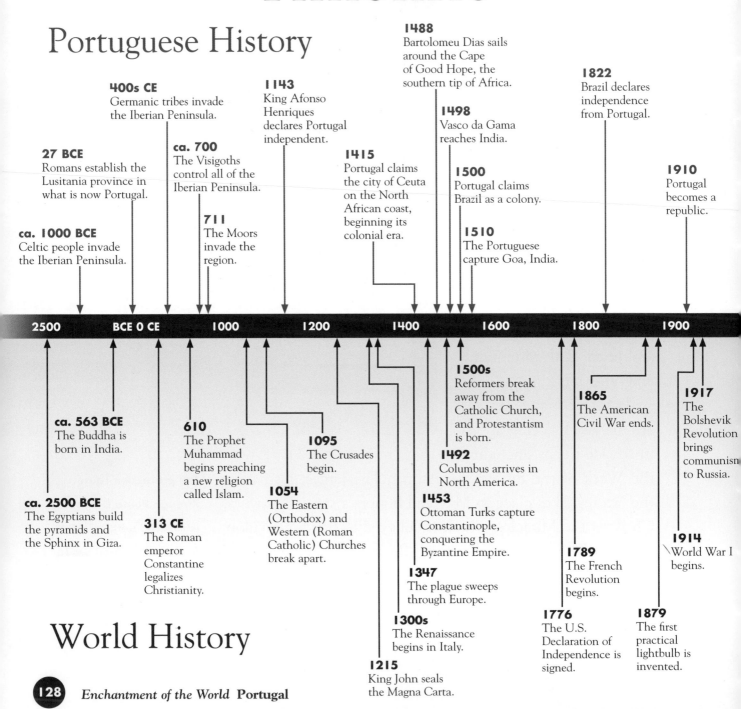

1488
Bartolomeu Dias sails
around the Cape
of Good Hope, the
southern tip of Africa.

400s CE
Germanic tribes invade
the Iberian Peninsula.

1143
King Afonso
Henriques
declares Portugal
independent.

1498
Vasco da Gama
reaches India.

1822
Brazil declares
independence
from Portugal.

27 BCE
Romans establish the
Lusitania province in
what is now Portugal.

ca. 700
The Visigoths
control all of the
Iberian Peninsula.

1415
Portugal claims
the city of Ceuta
on the North
African coast,
beginning its
colonial era.

1500
Portugal claims
Brazil as a colony.

1910
Portugal
becomes a
republic.

ca. 1000 BCE
Celtic people invade
the Iberian Peninsula.

711
The Moors
invade the
region.

1510
The Portuguese
capture Goa, India.

2500　　BCE 0 CE　　1000　　1200　　1400　　1600　　1800　　1900

ca. 563 BCE
The Buddha is
born in India.

610
The Prophet
Muhammad
begins preaching
a new religion
called Islam.

1095
The Crusades
begin.

1500s
Reformers break
away from the
Catholic Church,
and Protestantism
is born.

1865
The American
Civil War ends.

1917
The
Bolshevik
Revolution
brings
communism
to Russia.

ca. 2500 BCE
The Egyptians build
the pyramids and
the Sphinx in Giza.

1054
The Eastern
(Orthodox) and
Western (Roman
Catholic) Churches
break apart.

1492
Columbus arrives in
North America.

1453
Ottoman Turks capture
Constantinople,
conquering the
Byzantine Empire.

1914
World War I
begins.

313 CE
The Roman
emperor
Constantine
legalizes
Christianity.

1789
The French
Revolution
begins.

1347
The plague sweeps
through Europe.

World History

1300s
The Renaissance
begins in Italy.

1776
The U.S.
Declaration of
Independence is
signed.

1879
The first
practical
lightbulb is
invented.

1215
King John seals
the Magna Carta.

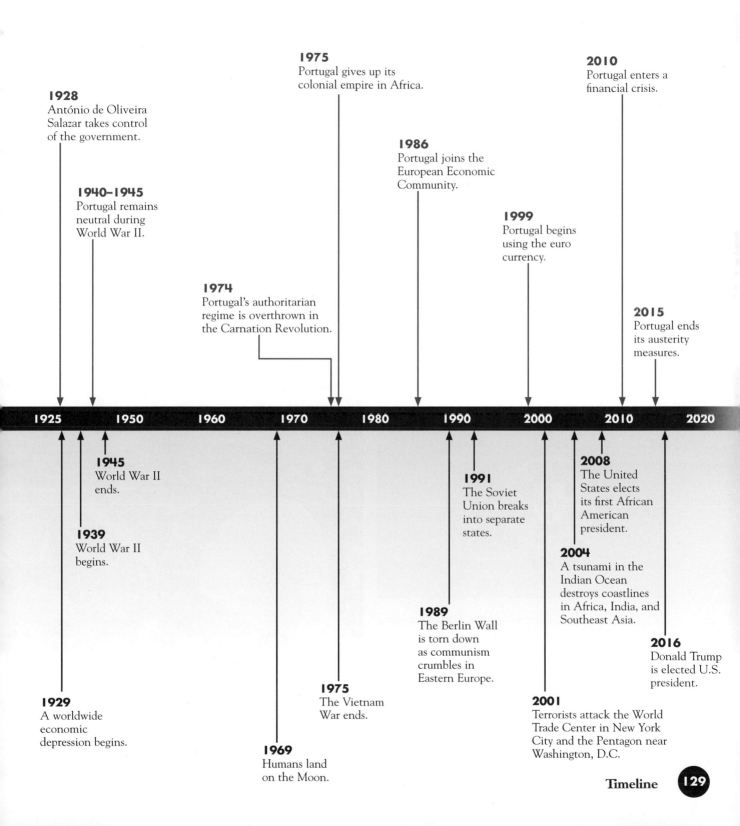

1928
António de Oliveira Salazar takes control of the government.

1940–1945
Portugal remains neutral during World War II.

1975
Portugal gives up its colonial empire in Africa.

1986
Portugal joins the European Economic Community.

2010
Portugal enters a financial crisis.

1999
Portugal begins using the euro currency.

1974
Portugal's authoritarian regime is overthrown in the Carnation Revolution.

2015
Portugal ends its austerity measures.

1925   1950   1960   1970   1980   1990   2000   2010   2020

1945
World War II ends.

1939
World War II begins.

1991
The Soviet Union breaks into separate states.

2008
The United States elects its first African American president.

2004
A tsunami in the Indian Ocean destroys coastlines in Africa, India, and Southeast Asia.

1929
A worldwide economic depression begins.

1989
The Berlin Wall is torn down as communism crumbles in Eastern Europe.

2016
Donald Trump is elected U.S. president.

1975
The Vietnam War ends.

1969
Humans land on the Moon.

2001
Terrorists attack the World Trade Center in New York City and the Pentagon near Washington, D.C.

Fast Facts

Official name of the country: Portuguese Republic

Capital: Lisbon

Official language: Portuguese

Official religion: None

Year of founding: 1143; republic proclaimed 1910

National anthem: "A Portuguesa" ("The Portuguese")

Type of government: Republic

Head of state: President

Head of government: Prime minister

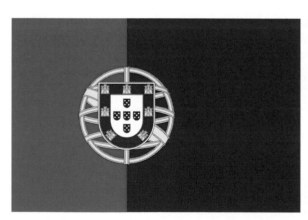

Left to right: **National flag, Changing of the Guard ceremony**

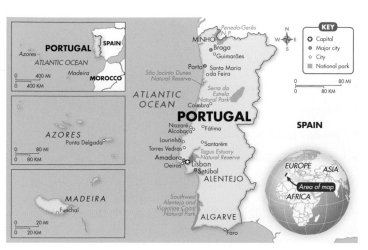

Beach in Algarve

Area of country: 35,603 square miles (92,212 sq km)

Bordering country: Spain to the north and east

Highest elevation: Mount Pico in the Azores, 7,713 feet (2,351 m)

Highest elevation on the mainland: Mount Torre, 6,539 feet (1,993 m)

Lowest elevation: Sea level along the coast

Longest river: Tagus, 171 miles (275 km)

Average high temperature: In Lisbon, 59°F (15°C) in January, 82°F (28°C) in July

Average low temperature: In Lisbon, 47°F (8°C) in January, 65°F (18°C) in July

Average annual precipitation: 20 to 80 inches (50 to 200 cm)

National population (2017):	10,308,488	
Population of major cities (2018 est.):	Lisbon	517,802
	Porto	249,633
	Amadora	178,858
	Braga	121,394
	Setúbal	117,110

Landmarks:
- ▶ *Belém Tower,* Lisbon
- ▶ *Braga Cathedral,* Braga
- ▶ *Monument to the Discoveries,* Lisbon
- ▶ *Peneda-Gerês National Park,* Braga
- ▶ *São Bento Railway Station,* Porto

Economy: Portugal manufacturers turn out automobiles, clothing, paper products, leather goods, medicines, and wine. Portugal is the world's leading producer of cork for wine bottles. Fishing is a major industry. Farmers grow grapes for wine and olives, which are turned into olive oil. Portugal is also an important producer of copper and tungsten. The nation has a thriving tourist industry, with visitors coming to surf, go whale watching, and tour historic sites. Technical industries are growing at a fast pace.

Currency: The euro. In 2018, 1 euro equaled $1.14, and $1.00 equaled 0.87 euros.

System of weights and measures: Metric system

Literacy rate: Nearly 100%

Portuguese words and phrases:	*Olá*	Hello
	Adeus	Good-bye
	Sim	Yes
	Não	No
	Faz favor	Please
	Obrigado	Thank you
	Bom dia	Good morning

Prominent Portuguese People:

Luís de Camões *Poet*	(ca. 1524–1580)
Bartolomeu Dias *Explorer*	(1450–1500)
Vasco da Gama *Explorer*	(ca. 1460–1524)
António Guterres *Diplomat*	(1949–)
Fernando Pessoa *Poet*	(1888–1935)
Amália Rodrigues *Singer*	(1920–1999)
José Saramago *Writer*	(1922–2010)

Clockwise from top: **Currency, Amália Rodrigues, schoolchildren**

To Find Out More

Books

▶ Bergreen, Laurence. *Magellan: Over the Edge of the World*. New York: Roaring Brook Press, 2017.

▶ DK Eyewitness Travel. *Portugal*. New York: DK Eyewitness Travel, 2018.

Music

▶ *The Best of Fado: Um Tesouro Português*. Lisbon: EMI Portugal, 2003.

▶ Rodrigues, Amália. *The Art of Amália: Her Greatest Recordings*. London: Parlophone, 1998.

▶ *The Rough Guide to the Music of Portugal*. London: World Music Network, 1998.

▶ Visit this Scholastic website for more information on Portugal:
www.factsfornow.scholastic.com
Enter the keyword **Portugal**

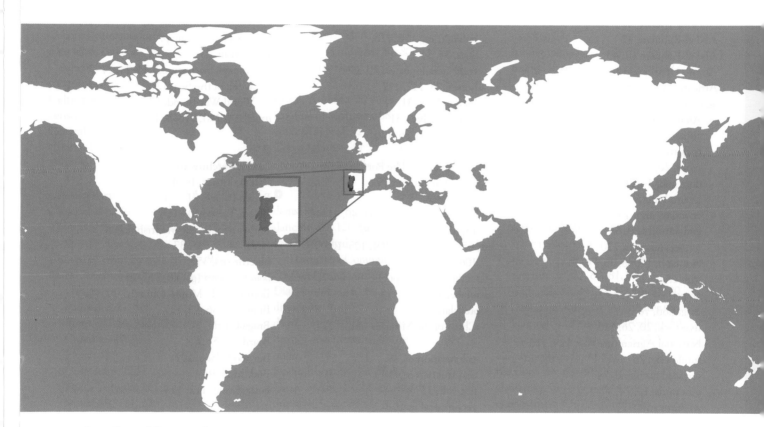

Location of Portugal

Meet the Authors

Ettagale Blauer and Jason Lauré have spent their careers exploring the world and writing about countries. Together, they have written roughly twenty books in Scholastic's Enchantment of the World series.

Each country has a unique personality. In Blauer's career as a journalist, gathering facts and impressions in various countries, she has particularly enjoyed Portugal, a country where history comes alive through the ancient buildings and monuments.

Photo Credits

Photographs ©: cover: Sean Pavone/iStockphoto; back cover: Enrique Díaz/7cero/Getty Images; 2: Nicolas Armer/Aurora Photos; 4 left: SeanPavonePhoto/iStockphoto; 4 center: Jan Wlodarczyk/Robert Harding Picture Library; 4 right: Martin Harvey/Getty Images; 5 left: J.M.F. Almeida/Getty Images; 5 right: Mauricio Abreu/Getty Images; 6: Marco Bottigelli/Getty Images; 9: Mary Evans Picture Library Ltd/age fotostock; 10: J.M.F. Almeida/Getty Images; 11: franz12/Shutterstock; 12: LordRunar/iStockphoto; 13: David Santiago Garcia/Aurora Photos; 14: Jan Wlodarczyk/Robert Harding Picture Library; 17: Tolo Balaguer/age fotostock; 18: Nicolas Armer/Aurora Photos; 19: FernandoAH/iStockphoto; 20: Heinz Wohner/LOOK Die Bildagentur der Fotografen GmbH/Alamy Images; 21: Jacek_Sopotnicki/iStockphoto; 22: Luca Quadrio/Alamy Images; 23: API/Gamma-Rapho/Getty Images; 24: Marshall Ikonography/Alamy Images; 25: Robert Seitz/imageBROKER/age fotostock; 26: Mauricio Abreu/Getty Images; 27 top right: Gosiek-B/iStockphoto; 27 bottom left: SeanPavonePhoto/iStockphoto; 28: Jose Pedro Fernandes/Alamy Images; 30: Mauricio Abreu/Getty Images; 31: Pete Oxford/Minden Pictures; 32: Pablo Blazquez Dominguez/Getty Images; 33: Günter Lenz/imageBROKER/age fotostock; 34 left: Adriano Bacchella/Minden Pictures; 34 right: Julia Christe/Getty Images; 35: Martin Harvey/Getty Images; 36: Nacho Doce/Reuters; 37: Jacobo Hernández/age fotostock; 38: Zoonar/N.Sorokin/age fotostock; 40: Oliver Strewe/Getty Images; 41: Christian Goupi/age fotostock; 43: Fine Art Images/age fotostock; 44: bpk Bildagentur/Art Resource, NY; 45: duncan1890/Getty Images; 47: DEA/G. Dagli Orti/Getty Images; 48: horstgerlach/iStockphoto; 50: Mary Evans Picture Library Ltd/age fotostock; 51: Heritage Image Partnership Ltd/Alamy Images; 52: /Alamy Images; 53: Harlingue/Roger Viollet/Getty Images; 54: ullstein bild/Getty Images; 55: Z1 Collection/Alamy Images; 56: Collection/Alamy Images; 57: Royal Air Force Official Photographer/IWM/Getty Images; 58: Horacio Villalobos/Corbis/Getty Images; 60: 111Jean-Claude Francolon/Gamma-Rapho/Getty Images; 61: Henri Bureau/Sygma/Corbis/Getty Images; 62: Keystone Pictures USA/Alamy Images; 63: Lucas Vallecillos/age fotostock; 64: Miguel Riopa/AFP/Getty Images; 65: Konrad Zelazowski/age fotostock; 66: Horacio Villalobos/Corbis/Getty Images; 69: Luiz Rampelotto/EuropaNewswire/age fotostock; 70: Jose Manuel Ribeiro/AFP/Getty Images; 71: www.victoriawlaka.com/Getty Images; 72: iangpv/iStockphoto; 73 top right: ESB Professional/Shutterstock; 74: Mauricio Abreu/AWL Images; 76: Mauricio Abreu/Getty Images; 78: Jeff Rotman/Getty Images; 80: Charles Stirling/Alamy Images; 81: Marco Bottigelli/AWL Images; 82: Mauricio Abreu/Getty Images; 83: CSP_paolo77/age fotostock; 84: Karol Kozlowski/age fotostock; 87: Patricia De Melo Moreira/AFP/Getty Images; 88: Martin Siepmann/age fotostock; 89: Carlos Sanchez Pereyra/AWL Images; 90: Sergio Azenha/Alamy Images; 91: DimaBerkut/iStockphoto; 92: Mauricio Abreu/AWL Images; 94: 932923Carlos Costa/NurPhoto/Getty Images; 95: Tatiana Popova/Shutterstock; 96 left: Mary Evans Picture Library Ltd/age fotostock; 96 right: Francisco Leong/AFP/Getty Images; 97: Nick Ledger/Getty Images; 98: Pablo Blazquez Dominguez/Getty Images; 99: Pablo Méndez/age fotostock; 100: Endless Travel/Alamy Images; 102: Cro Magnon/Alamy Images; 103: Manuel Litran/Paris Match/Getty Images; 104: Paul Bernhardt/Getty Images; 105: DEA Picture Library/age fotostock; 106: Peter Horree/Alamy Images; 107: Mark Avellino/Getty Images; 108: Mauricio Abreu/Getty Images; 109: Graziano Arici/age fotostock; 110: Martin Thomas Photography/Alamy Images; 111: Phil Cole/Getty Images/Getty Images; 112: Carol Walker/Minden Pictures; 113: Patricia De Melo Moreira/AFP/Getty Images; 114: Neil Farrin/AWL Images; 116: PeopleImages/Getty Images; 117: Stuart Dee/Getty Images; 118: Egon Bömsch/imageBROKER/age fotostock; 119: Martin Moxter/age fotostock; 120: Jan Wlodarczyk/Alamy Images; 121: Stefano Baldini/age fotostock; 122: 88833Horacio Villalobos/Corbis/Getty Images; 123: Thorsten Suedfels/Picture Press/Getty Images; 124: Zoonar/URF/age fotostock; 125: Mauricio Abreu/Getty Images; 126: THEGIFT777/iStockphoto; 127: Walter Bibikow/AWL Images; 130 left: iangpv/iStockphoto; 130 right: www.victoriawlaka.com/Getty Images; 131 right: Marco Bottigelli/AWL Images; 133 center left: CSP_paolo77/age fotostock; 133 bottom left: Sergio Azenha/Alamy Images; 133 bottom right: Manuel Litran/Paris Match/Getty Images.

Maps by Mapping Specialists.